UNLIKELY
COMPANIONS

UNLIKELY COMPANIONS

The Adventures of an Exotic Animal Doctor
(or, What Friends Feathered, Furred, and Scaled
Have Taught Me About Life and Love)

DR. LAURIE HESS,
DVM, Diplomate ABVP (Avian Practice) Exotic Animal Veterinarian

WITH SAMANTHA ROSE

DA CAPO PRESS

Designed by Linda Mark
Set in 12.25 point Weiss Std by the Perseus Books Group

Library of Congress Cataloging-in-Publication Data
Names: Hess, Laurie, author.
Title: Unlikely companions : the adventures of an exotic animal veterinarian (or, what friends feathered, furred, and scaled have taught me about life and love) / Dr. Laurie Hess, DVM, Diplomate AVBP (Avian) Exotic Animal Veterinarian, with Samantha Rose.
Description: First Da Capo Press edition. | Boston : Da Capo Press, 2016. |
    Includes bibliographical references.
Identifiers: LCCN 2016024797 (print) | LCCN 2016035439 (ebook) (print) |
    LCCN 2016035440 (ebook) | ISBN 9780738219578 (hardcover) |
    ISBN 9780738219585 (e-book)
Subjects: LCSH: Exotic animals—Diseases—Anecdotes. | Pet medicine—Anecdotes. |
    Hess, Laurie.
Classification: LCC SF997.5.E95 H47 2016b (print) | LCC SF997.5.E95 (ebook) |
    DDC 636.089—dc23
LC record available at https://lccn.loc.gov/2016024797

First Da Capo Press edition 2016
Published by Da Capo Press, an imprint of Perseus Books, LLC, a subsidiary of Hachette Book Group, Inc.
www.dacapopress.com

Da Capo Press books are available at special discounts for bulk purchases in the U.S. by corporations, institutions, and other organizations. For more information, please contact the Special Markets Department at the Perseus Books Group, 2300 Chestnut Street, Suite 200, Philadelphia, PA, 19103, or call (800) 810-4145, ext. 5000, or e-mail special.markets@perseusbooks.com.

10 9 8 7 6 5 4 3 2 1

NOTE TO READERS

This story is based on real events. Except for the names of Dr. Hess' family members, the names and some identifying characteristics of the other people and companies mentioned in this book have been changed.

To all the birds and exotic animals
and the owners who love and care for them.

CONTENTS

1

A MYSTERIOUS CASE

MONDAY, 4:28 A.M., HOME

I got the call in what felt like the middle of the night.

"He's dead, Laurie," said my head technician, Marnie.

I threw back the quilt and scurried out of bed and down the hallway, cell phone in hand. I was careful not to wake my husband, Peter, who had gotten into bed only a few hours before, back from a long week of providing legal counsel on the other side of the country.

The uneven floor creaked in our center-hall colonial. Through the narrow four-paned window at the top of the stairs, I could barely make out the tangle of naked maple trees in our almost pitch-black backyard.

My cell phone confirmed that it was early: 4:28 a.m. As a local vet, I keep the same hours as many of the farmers in my community do. At five o'clock every morning, the reassuring aroma of espresso roast makes its way upstairs, but at this hour, the kitchen was still and quiet.

"I found him in his incubator this morning," Marnie said. "And I just received a call from Bob Dixon. He wants to bring in Lily. The symptoms are the same, and I fear the worst. How quickly can you be at the hospital?"

This was the fourth death in less than ten days, and, like Marnie, I'd been holding my breath, worried that there might be more. Now she'd confirmed that we'd lost another, and Lily was sick. I wouldn't have time to wait for my first cup of coffee.

"I'm on my way."

I hurried to get dressed, pulling on workout clothes over my insulin pump, then my knee-high leather Frye boots and Marmot down jacket, the winter uniform of country and not-so-country vets far and wide. A quick check of my blood sugar—I have type 1 diabetes—told me that I had to eat before rushing off, so, accompanied by my four cats, Bingo, Gizmo, Tilly, and Bean, who thought I'd gotten up to feed them, I tiptoed on the wide-planked pine floors through our dark farmhouse and into the kitchen, nearly falling over a mountain of bags. I'm constantly on my middle school sons, Brett and Luke, for creating an obstacle course of boyhood gear wherever they go, but this time the mess was my own—pelleted bird food that I myself had brought home for our pionus parrot, Dale. So I really couldn't complain. Our house had been named "Applewood" when it was originally built as the groomsman's house on an estate; now we simply called it the "Hess-Mess."

Because Peter had been out of town, the fridge was emptier than usual, as he's our main provisioner. I settled for a string cheese in one pocket and an apple in the other and scampered out the door, down the flagstone path to the driveway. The sun was not yet rising, and it would be several hours before the ground thawed. Winter temperatures had dropped below twenty degrees overnight, and a thin sheet of ice covered my

Highlander windshield, a good indicator that the air was frigid. With mittened hands clutching the ice scraper, I removed the ice from the windows quickly but with surgical precision. The hospital is only seven minutes from home, so, if I hurried, I might make it back before the school bus arrived. It was Monday morning, and with Peter still on West Coast time, I regretted leaving him to rouse the boys single-handedly and get them out the door.

I found Marnie in the intensive care unit of the animal hospital wearing her scrubs and carefully tagging the body.

"Good morning," I whispered as I slipped in. I didn't want to startle her, but I did.

She turned quickly and said, "That was fast. You're already here."

I extended a coffee from Starbucks, which—thankfully for us—opens its doors at 5 a.m. She gave me a tired smile and took the oversized cup from my hands. I was grateful to Marnie for staying overnight at the hospital. When she offered, I'd initially declined, because overnights were not standard practice. But given the seriousness of the case and the need for round-the-clock supportive care, I'd finally decided it was a good idea.

"Peter's back from Los Angeles now, so I can take over."

She looked down at the body. "I was sure he was going to make it, but he stopped responding to the antibiotics early this morning." Her voice trailed off. Marnie doesn't give in to emotion easily, but she was taking this especially hard. Of course she cares about all of our patients, as I do, and sometimes you make an especially strong connection with certain animals. Georgie had been one of them.

"It's not your fault, Marnie. We both tried everything."

I walked over to the exam table where she'd laid the five-inch body out on a clean white towel. I reached down and stroked Georgie's velvety fur. With his doe-shaped eyes closed and long puffy tail wrapped around him, the sugar glider looked as if he were simply cuddled up for a warm winter's nap. I ran a finger down the black stripe on Georgie's back and imagined the little marsupial sailing through the air, wide-eyed and gleeful as he jumped from branch to branch in his milder native Australian habitat. The fold, or flap, of skin that stretches from their front toes to their ankles enables these unique animals to sail through the air. I thought of him catching the breeze, as light as a kite in the wind.

But now Georgie lay there looking both extinguished and newborn at the same time. I remembered how as babies, Brett and Luke had slept peacefully in their hospital bassinettes in those first few hours of life, with Peter and me peering down on them with that delight and wonder that all new parents must feel. I thought about Georgie's own mother. How had she looked at him on that first night of his arrival, as he lay snuggled in her pouch?

Georgie was a doll, a bright and playful little creature. And though I'd treated many sugar gliders in recent years, none had been quite as young and slight as Georgie. He was just over a month out of pouch and could fit into the palm of a child's hand.

"I really hoped he'd be the one to bounce back, too," I said, smiling wearily at Marnie. "When I left the hospital last night, I thought, maybe tomorrow's the day he makes a sudden recovery and leaps into my arms. But he was just so young and vulnerable. Like the others, he got too weak, too fast, to recover."

"Would you like me to phone Maxine?" Marnie asked.

When an animal dies at the hospital without its owner pres-ent, we must make what is always a difficult call. First, we have to deliver the news that no pet owner wants to hear, and then we need to discuss what the owner wants us to do with the body. Many owners want to bury their own pets; others ask us to cremate them. As we comply with their wishes, we also collect something from their pet—a lock of hair, a few feath-ers, or a footprint—that we pass along in a sympathy card. I noticed now that an impression of Georgie's tiny webbed toes was already on a card taped to the back counter of the ICU, the ink imprint smaller than my thumbnail. Marnie's signature was the first on it.

As the head tech of the hospital, Marnie often has the responsibility of being the first line of communication with clients, but considering the overnight hours she'd just logged and the nature of the message, I offered to call Georgie's owner. Then I said, "Why don't you take a break while you can."

I took a deep breath. Georgie's death was only the first order of business today. I had appointments booked solid: an umbrella cockatoo, a chinchilla, a blue-tongued skink, a preg-nant potbellied pig, and a ferret possibly needing surgery. I often jest that while an exotic pet hospital is very different from a zoo, on Monday mornings it sure can feel like one.

As I have with my own home, I've created this menagerie of managed chaos; so again, I have no one to blame but myself. As far as I know, I'm the only exotic pet veterinarian in the tristate area who offers emergency phone consultations—at midnight, on weekends, or even, as my kids like to remind me, when we're walking through the Magic Kingdom on vacation.

My phone starts to buzz as soon as I close the hospital doors late Saturday afternoon with calls from frantic pet owners asserting "health emergencies." Most of the time, the descriptions sound perfectly benign, so I'll say something like, "I understand your concern. Right now, this doesn't sound quite like an emergency, but if you're still really concerned, I can send you to the emergency hospital for an evaluation by the on-duty veterinarian. Otherwise, I suggest you monitor your pet over the weekend, and on Monday morning, call me back." Most of the time, I don't get a call back. A crowd of exotic pet owners shows up in the hospital lobby instead. A week ago on Monday, I walked through the door at a quarter to nine and was greeted by a spiny hedgehog with gastrointestinal issues that his eleven-year-old owner insisted could not wait another minute. "He's got really *bad* farts," the boy said, making a stink face. "Please make it stop."

This morning I expected to find the owner of an orange-and-white Creamsicle-looking corn snake in the waiting room as soon as the clock struck nine. I'd received her insistent call Saturday night just after I'd said goodnight to the boys and was heading downstairs to pour myself a glass of my favorite New Zealand sauvignon blanc, flip on the evening news, and start combing through veterinary journals online. Never a down moment, I thought to myself, but because I understand that finding a vet after hours for a Labrador retriever or a tabby cat is hard enough, I always answer the call.

"Hello, this is Dr. Hess," I said, running a hand through my dark, curly hair. My hair is difficult to control even at a normal hour, but at that time of night, it's lawless. "How can I help you?"

"My daughter's snake, Cutie, crawled into her dollhouse and got stuck." The caller had a note of panic in her voice. "I can't get her out."

Well, at least this one's still visible, I thought. Usually when a snake goes missing, it stays that way. Pet snakes love to disappear into the walls of our homes through cracks, holes, and pipes or under the floorboards. When that happens they're almost never seen again. To a pet snake that spends his days and nights confined to a forty-gallon terrarium, wandering off is tempting once it gets out. Our homes hold the promise of freedom, of a grand adventure, except that the deeper they get into a labyrinth of hidden places, the more lost they get.

I'd first heard about a missing snake when I was working as a resident veterinarian at the Animal Medical Center in Manhattan.

"DID I TELL you I found my python?" my intern, Lauren, had asked me.

Lauren's missing ball python, Cecil, had been the topic of much conversation in the surgery room. Ball pythons are a very popular pet snake, especially in apartments because they rarely grow longer than five or six feet and do not get very wide in girth—except they commonly go missing, often for months or even years at a time. I'd gone over to Lauren's twenty-two-story high-rise in Midtown Manhattan, where many of the interns lived, to try to help find the brown-and-gold-speckled snake, but after a thorough search we conceded that he seemed to have disappeared without a trace. After several months, Lauren had given up on ever seeing him again.

"Where'd you find him?"

"Oh, *I* didn't—another tenant did. My neighbor Jill got into the elevator, and there he was. Curled up in a tight little ball in the middle of the elevator floor. Pretty fantastic, right?"

Lauren was beaming, but I couldn't help wondering if "fantastic" in this situation was a relative term. I doubted that Jill shared Lauren's enthusiasm when she stepped into the elevator and found a four-foot python at her feet.

As if she'd heard my thoughts, Lauren chortled, "Well, I guess it did freak her out a little bit. She said she felt something touch her foot and ignored it until Cecil uncurled and started crawling up her leg. She screamed, kicked him off, and ran out of the elevator so fast, she said, that she left her strappy sandal behind." Lauren giggled to herself. "Oh, Cecil, he doesn't mean any harm."

I imagined that Cecil must have survived for all those months on the building's rodent population, but I didn't share that conclusion with Lauren, since she still lived there. Stumbling upon a food source is the best-case scenario for a lost snake like Cecil, although snakes can survive for long periods without any food at all. They will curl up and go into a sort of shutdown mode, in which they slow their heartbeat, lower their temperature, and stop moving. Their already slow metabolism comes to a near standstill, and they can survive without food much longer than most any other animal I know of. I remembered my client Gus, the owner of a red, brown, and yellow milk snake that was about three inches in girth and went missing for nearly a year. Like Lauren, Gus had thought he'd never see his pet again, but the snake must have been living in the pipes behind his fridge. One morning, he slithered out of his hiding place, and Gus stumbled on him in the middle of the floor. Looking rather emaciated and weak, like a deflated bicycle tire, the snake was in desperate need of emergency care, so Gus gently coiled him up and transported him to our hospital in the bottom of a laundry basket. There I treated him for extreme dehydration with a dose of an electrolyte solution under his skin and some liquid food through a tube passed down to his stomach.

I shook aside my memories of Cecil and Gus and calmly returned to the after-hours call. "How long has Cutie been in the dollhouse?"

"I guess . . . it's been about two weeks now?"

I sat down and poured myself that glass of wine. I thought, Cutie's been inside the dollhouse for more than two weeks, but right now, at eleven-thirty on a Saturday night, her owner has decided it's finally time she move out.

"Does the snake appear to be hurt or in any pain?" I asked.

"Uh"—she paused again—"what would pain look like?"

"That's a good question. It's the difference between looking restful and frustrated. Does Cutie appear to be struggling, like she's trying to get free?"

"Not really," she replied. "She's curled up in a ball in the master bedroom. I think she's asleep."

I took a sip of sauv blanc.

"And I'm sure she's not hungry," she continued. "I've been putting food on the front porch for her to eat."

Just as I'd suspected, as with many of the distressed emergency calls I get from exotic pet owners late at night, Cutie did not need emergency care. She was already getting the best care right where she was. For two weeks she'd been checked into the best reptile bed-and-breakfast in town.

Her owner asked, "So what should I do?"

"Stop feeding her, and then on Monday, if Cutie still hasn't checked out, call me back."

7:15 A.M., VETERINARY CENTER FOR BIRDS & EXOTICS

I LEFT THE ICU with Georgie's chart and walked back to my office. I looked at the wall clock. We had just under an hour before the hospital opened to the crush of another busy Monday morning. I was going to need more coffee. I sank down in my Ikea desk chair and positioned myself in front of the phone. Veterinarians may joke that we become animal doctors so that we don't have to deal with people, but that isn't at all the case. Veterinary medicine is as much about building human relationships as about treating animals. When Maxine had brought her nearly lifeless glider into the hospital on Friday, I had seen immediately from the dark circles beneath her eyes that this distraught owner was going to need care and attention too.

Maxine was cupping the limp glider in her hands. "Please help him," she pleaded. "I don't know what to do. He's hardly moving." I gently wrapped Georgie in a soft towel and set him down on the examining table. Before handling pets at the hospital, I wrap them this way. It keeps them from scratching me or wiggling away. Like human babies, most animals like the security and comfort of being swaddled in a towel. I wrapped up Georgie, but I could tell from his spiritless behavior that he wasn't going anywhere. His big, dark eyes were uncharacteristically droopy for a sugar glider, not at all bright or wide. Usually, the large eyes of a sugar glider, disproportionate to their small bodies, remind me of ET, the extraterrestrial in the Steven Spielberg film.

I opened Georgie's mouth. His tongue and gums were dehydrated and dry, and his breathing was labored and shallow, his chest barely moving.

"I did everything they told me to," Maxine said and pulled a pamphlet out of her Coach Classic tote. She unfolded "How to Care for a Sugar Glider" on the table in front of me and pointed to the third bullet point: hand feeding. "I even tried feeding him mealworms by hand. Can you imagine *me* doing that?"

I gave her a reassuring smile.

"Still," she said, "he couldn't keep any food down without shaking."

Maxine was shaking now too.

"I really didn't mean for him to get sick."

"I'm sure you did everything right," I said.

Guilt. I run into this animal every day at the hospital. Nearly every pet owner brings in some amount of it. Georgie had gotten sick, and Maxine was blaming herself. *I should have seen the signs. I should have caught it earlier. I shouldn't have waited. What was I thinking?* In all my years of veterinary practice, I have met few pet owners who don't feel a deep, personal responsibility for their pets' health and happiness, and when their animals get sick, they blame themselves for somehow failing them. Maxine began to cry.

"I should have known better," she said. "Jesus, what do I know about taking care of a sugar glider?" She wiped the corners of her eyes. "I didn't even know what one was until two weeks ago." She took a deep breath and regained her composure.

"I was visiting my sister in Connecticut," she said. "We were out shopping at the mall, and they were selling them right outside Macy's, of all places. Out of nowhere, here comes this little animal flying through the air toward me. He landed right on my shoulder. He was the most adorable thing, and I fell in love right away. I would have tucked him into my purse and taken him with me that minute, but the company spokesman asked me to think on it and revisit the mall in two days. If I still wanted Georgie, then I could fill out all the necessary paperwork, complete the adoption process, and take him home. They do this, they say, to discourage impulse buys. Well, after coming up with every possible reason I could think of not to go back to the mall and adopt Georgie, of course I did."

From my office, I dialed Maxine's number. She picked up after the first ring.

"Good morning, Maxine. It's Dr. Hess from the Veterinary Center for Birds & Exotics."

She took a deep breath. "It's early. It must be bad news."

I hesitated. Delivering news of a death is by far the hardest part of my job, and even though I've offered my condolences many more times than I'd like to count, I regret doing it every time. There's no really easy way to pass on news of a death. I've learned that a direct approach is less painful to receive.

"I'm sorry, Maxine. It's not good news. We did everything we could, but Georgie was very sick. Despite our best efforts, Georgie has passed away."

Maxine was quiet.

"I'm very sorry," I said again.

She choked. "I understand."

I knew she must be feeling guilty all over again, so I said, "Please understand that this isn't your fault. You took great care of Georgie. There's nothing you did to make Georgie sick."

"Then what *did*?" she asked in a pained whisper.

If only I knew. I didn't have an answer for her. Not a complete one anyway.

"Georgie died of organ failure early this morning, and we're still trying to determine the cause. As soon as I know more, you'll be the first person I call."

What had made Georgie sick was still a mystery to me—as were the deaths of the three other young gliders that had died before him. I replayed the events of the last ten days in my mind.

When the first lethargic glider had shown up at the hospital, I wasn't too concerned. Gliders are naturally energetic and sometimes so high intensity in their activity that they easily exhaust themselves. But extreme weakness is typically the result of quick-onset malnutrition—a condition that exotic animal vets see in sugar gliders all the time. As someone with adult-onset diabetes, I can immediately recognize the signs. A glider is most often suffering from a poor diet if he has the shakes, similar to how I feel when my blood sugar levels swing out of whack. Some pet owners don't know that, despite what their name suggests, sugar gliders actually need a balanced diet rich in calcium and protein to maintain their bounce-off-the-walls vibrancy. When fed a diet high in fruits and sugary vegetables, they get sick—just as humans do—and end up with deficiencies in calcium, vitamins, and protein, putting them at risk for rickets and bone fractures. Sure, sugar gliders love sugar. They'll happily eat grapes, berries, and bananas all day long, and in the wild they also use their large incisor teeth to chew on the branches of trees, such as apple and citrus, from which they extract sweet sap. But fruits should really only make up 20 to 25 percent of their total diet. I recommend that at least 50 percent of their diet come from a commercially prepared and balanced pelleted food, which should be supplemented with proteins, such as hard-cooked egg yolks or insects.

I recalled the reaction of a young girl who'd brought in her sugar glider for a routine checkup when I told her, "Your glider needs a combination of nutrient-rich foods. You can continue to feed your glider some fruit, but," I said, teasing her, "be sure to sprinkle some bugs on top. Crickets and mealworms are your sugar glider's favorite. He'll gobble them right up."

"Eeew," she said with easy disgust. I smiled and assured both her and her mother that pelleted food containing essential protein, nutrients, and vitamins was also available at their local pet store. "You don't have to collect the bugs yourself." I held out a starter bag for the girl to take home. She clung to her mother's side. I bent down and whispered in her ear. "Not to worry. I already checked it. Nothing crawling in this one."

When I'd examined the first sick glider ten days ago, I'd thought I was seeing the telltale signs of a poor diet, which is fairly straightforward to treat. I prescribed oral calcium supplementation and a syringe feeding formula to boost vitamin D levels, minerals, and protein. Even when the second sick glider came in a day later with the same symptoms and the third a day after that, I wasn't overly concerned. I followed with a similar treatment plan and placed each sick glider in an incubator in the ICU to help regulate its body temperature. I was confident they'd all show signs of recovery fairly quickly. I had seen dozens of gliders over the past several years with similar signs, and all of them had recovered with supportive care and proper nutrition.

But when X-ray and blood test results for these three sick gliders came back from the lab, they showed normal sugar, calcium, and protein levels. At that point I got very concerned. If they're not malnourished, I wondered, then what is making them sick? Could they have some strange infection? Was something in their environment—their houses or apartments or water or food—affecting them all, even though they lived in different homes?

Marnie and I administered a series of antibiotics, anti-inflammatory medications, and additional nutritional supplements to all three animals, the type of general supportive treatment we usually administer to malnourished gliders. It's also what we give gliders with illnesses that we can't immediately identify. But with each passing hour, the little animals' conditions worsened. Each day, they became weaker and weaker. Whenever they attempted to climb, as they usually did, they would strain at the effort, struggling to pull their frail little bodies up the sides of their cages. Eventually they stopped trying. And then, horribly, they became unable to move at all and lay motionless on the bottoms of their cages. They wouldn't take mealworms or crickets—typically their favorite treats—and no medications or dietary supplements helped them improve. As their condition continued to worsen, they lost the ability even to swallow; the gruel we repeatedly tried to feed them through syringes just dribbled back out of their mouths.

With Georgie's death, I'd now lost four gliders. Nothing I'd done for any of these poor animals had worked. After two decades of practice, I wondered, how could I not find the answers? I'd always managed to do so before and to save gliders and other animal patients, especially with the help of all the technological advances, breakthrough studies, and new research that had allowed veterinary medicine to nearly catch up with human medicine. I'd learned how to do it all—operate on a chinchilla, medicate a tree frog, and treat respiratory infections in a parakeet—each time with the clock ticking and the animal's health hanging in the balance. What was I missing here?

I logged onto Vets Connect, a national resource site and online chat group for veterinarians far and wide. I'd been checking it for several days now, searching for answers and soliciting help. "If anybody sees similar symptoms," I'd asked, "please contact me immediately." So far, I hadn't received one response or seen a report. Until today. The top posting on the message board read, "Young sugar glider deaths."

I exhaled. I wasn't alone.

The top post describing a young female glider sounded eerily familiar. "A female sugar glider, Misty, with a 36-hour history of not wanting to eat and extreme lethargy. She is severely dehydrated with her most remarkable sign being throwing her head back and flailing her front legs whenever she is handled."

Tremors. Similar to what I'd seen in Georgie.

"The glider did not eat at all Monday," the report continued, "and Tues morning was extremely lethargic, just lying in her cage. Unfortunately Misty passed away today."

I anxiously scanned through the thread of comments underneath. There'd been two similar sugar glider deaths in Massachusetts. Another in Connecticut. More reports from Michigan. And Tampa. My stomach did a somersault. Adding them up, I got a death count of more than twenty. So the sickness wasn't isolated to my hospital. It was spreading across the country. In every case, frantic glider owners were showing up with their sick pets at clinics and animal hospitals. Just as I'd seen myself, their animals had suddenly become too ill to move, almost overnight.

Vets across the country were reporting the same symptoms I'd treated: extreme fatigue and muscle weakness, followed by tremors, seizures, and ultimately organ failure. From what I was reading, they were attempting to treat the gliders as I had—with antibiotics, anti-inflammatories, fluids, and nutritional supplements. But nothing was working. I read a post from Michigan stating that supportive care had been 50 percent successful and noting that the sick gliders improved initially but eventually succumbed. The necropsy report attached to this post read, "Vague changes to the kidney tubules, breakdown of liver tissue, and inflammation of the nerves. No obvious organisms or infectious agents seen."

I hadn't performed a necropsy on any of the four gliders that had died under my care. If Maxine permitted, I'd perform one on little Georgie. Perhaps it would tell me more than the general blood tests had revealed so far. I'd have to send the organ samples to our chief pathologist in California, who was familiar with sugar glider anatomy and illnesses. The results of a pathologist's report can sometimes take up to a week to get back. I'd just have to wait, fingers crossed, and hope that if another sick glider came through my hospital doors, it would have the strength to hold on.

My cell phone vibrated with a text from Marnie: "Bob Dixon—waiting room." That could only mean that another sick glider had arrived. I quickly unwrapped a protein bar and took a bite to keep my own blood sugar stable before heading to the front of the hospital.

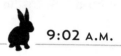 **9:02 A.M.**

MARNIE HAD THROWN the oversized burgundy doormat, imprinted with the hospital logo, outside the front door—an indication that the hospital was now open for business. I was amazed to see the waiting room still empty, except for Bob Dixon, who stood up to greet me from the cushioned bench that spanned the front window. I'd recognize him anywhere— lean and tall, dressed in a clean denim work shirt and cowboy boots. He extended a permanently stained hand, the result of years of finishing furniture he built from salvaged redwood, cedar, and white oak.

"Thanks for seeing me in a pinch, Dr. Hess," he said.

"Of course." I squeezed his hand. "Anything for Lily."

Bob's sugar glider Lily, who was quietly curled up in a corner of a small metal cage, had been a regular patient of mine for nearly five years.

"Why don't you bring her back to the examination room, and we'll take a look." I motioned toward an open door.

As soon as the door clicked shut, Bob set down the cage and then untucked his denim button-down, revealing yet another sugar glider nesting in the pocket of his white undershirt. I drew in a surprised breath. That Bob was "wearing" another animal was not unusual; it was standard practice for owners of these small marsupials. In fact, I had many clients with small pets who also preferred to keep them close. Cherie Marino always carried her beloved blue and yellow budgies, Lolly and

Molly, in her double-D bra and made a big presentation of rousing the small, chirpy birds from their human nest.

"Wake up, sleepyheads," she'd coo into the depths of her warm cleavage. Molly, the more gregarious of the two, whose feathers were a bright yellow, was always the first to peek out. She'd perch between the cups of Cherie's bra, chirping and observing her surroundings before jumping out. Lolly, the powder blue male bird, was more reserved and often needed coaxing out of his hiding place.

"Come on, Mister," Cherie would say. "Time to greet the world." She'd reach her hand between her breasts and scoop out Lolly, much like a magician pulling a rabbit from a hat.

Similarly to Mrs. Marino's budgerigars, marsupials like Bob Dixon's glider love the sensation and secure bond created by being physically close to their owners. They have a cozy, nesting nature, and snuggling inside Bob's warm shirt pocket probably felt a lot like being carried around by Mama in her pouch. In fact, many product designers have catered to these animals' desire to snuggle up. At the last pet product trade show I attended, among the thousands of booths exhibiting every type of product for every species of animal imaginable, the sugar glider "bonding pouch" worn around the neck like a little hammock or a baby sling was the clear winner—it had become more popular than the potbellied pig Björn and the ferret Pop-N-Play.

Despite these many options for pouches, however, Bob chose the simplicity of his shirt pocket.

"This is unexpected," I said. "When did Lily get . . . a sister?"

Bob smiled ever so slightly.

"Meet Mathilda." Bob reached inside his shirt pocket and retrieved a sweet little lump of fur—the tiniest glider I'd ever seen in my practice, even more petite than Georgie. "Today's her one-month birthday, thirty days old." He stroked the black stripe of fur that ran along her back.

Mathilda had a perfectly pink nose and charcoal eyelids, and as I took her from Bob's large, outstretched hand, she appeared even more fragile and slight. As I cupped her in my own, she remained unmoving with eyes closed. There was no mistaking that this baby glider, no longer than my ring finger, was sick.

"I'm going to examine her, and we'll go from there, okay?"

"Sure thing," Bob nodded.

From where she lay in her cage on the floor, Lily forced open one groggy eye and looked up at Bob in weak protest.

"You want to be held, too? " he asked. Bob bent down, unlatched the metal cage, and scooped Lily up. She snuggled against Bob and closed her eyes, as if the slightest movement exhausted her.

This was a noticeable change in Lily since the last time I'd seen her for a routine checkup. Then she had been so full of boundless energy that I'd had a hard time examining her. When she wasn't perched on Bob's shoulder, she was scrambling up and down his brawny arm. Whenever I'd reach for her, she'd cling to the fabric of his shirt, and it was nearly impossible to pry her off. At one of my attempts to pick her up, she'd leapt into the air and landed on my head.

Lily wasn't the only animal drawn to my nest of curls. It was such an attraction to pets in my practice that Marnie had suggested a photo stream on our hospital's website called Laurie's Locks, depicting a variety of animals burrowing in my hair. Even I had to admit that the family of canaries perched atop my head was well worth capturing.

"Where did you get Mathilda?" I asked, slowly stroking her fur.

"I thought it was time Lily finally got a playmate. Sort of like an early Christmas present," he answered, smiling slightly with embarrassment.

"That's rather sentimental of you," I gently teased.

"I'm a sucker. You already know that. I was walking through the mall on my way to Sears to replace my drill bits and get a new sander, and anyway, there was this guy selling baby gliders at a booth."

Sugar gliders hadn't become popular only because they were novel and cute; they were also relatively affordable and available nearly everywhere. I'd seen them for sale at the type of pop-up booths Maxine and now Bob were describing and also listed on Craigslist and eBay.

"You once told me that pet gliders are happiest in pairs and that single gliders get lonely."

"Because they're naturally social creatures," I said. "Yes, that's right."

He looked down at Lily and smoothed back the fur between her little ears. "That always stuck with me. Over the years I'd think about getting a second glider to keep her company, but then I never did. When I spotted Mathilda—I don't know, there was just something about her—I felt like I'd finally found the perfect companion for my girl."

I shined a light into Mathilda's tiny ears. They were free of discharge and debris. I used a Q-tip to look into her mouth. As she chewed on the soft cotton end, I smiled at Bob. "You did good. She's very sweet."

As I gently palpated Mathilda's abdomen, I asked, "When did you notice the first signs of sickness?"

He scratched his head and thought for a moment. "I brought her home five days ago, and everything was fine. She was full of life. Very energetic. Playful at night."

He was describing typical sugar glider behavior. Nocturnal creatures with huge eyes that function better in dim light, captive gliders are most active at night. Most glider owners wearily report that their pets jump from perch to perch and climb the walls of their cages way beyond a suitable bedtime for humans.

"Yesterday I noticed her movements were slow and she wasn't interested in her food, and then last night she began to have tremors."

"And Lily?"

"Stronger than Mathilda, but also lethargic. Lying around in her cage. When she didn't get up to eat this morning, I knew something was wrong with both of them."

Both of them sick? I was perplexed. All of the gliders that had recently died in my care were babies. But Lily was nearly five years old.

"What are you feeding them?"

"Mealworms, some hard-boiled egg, veggies, and pelleted food with just a little bit of nectar mix."

I could have hugged him for being so conscientious about his pets' diet. I educate pet owners about the importance of proper care all day long—at my hospital, at seminars, and in any forum where anyone will listen. I stress that exotic pets deserve exceptional care, and I hammer home the same simple message: learn what your pet needs and give him or her exactly that. Over the years, that's become my mantra.

The unfortunate reality is that nearly every day I meet pet owners who aren't providing proper care for their animals.

When I examine their pets, I can tell quickly that they are not feeding, sheltering, or caring for their animals in the most optimal way. It isn't intentional, of course; many pet owners simply lack the correct information. And it's no wonder. Even a couple of decades ago, there was little scientifically based medical knowledge available about how to properly care for exotic pets, especially when compared with cats and dogs. If even veterinary schools don't have complete information on the care of exotics, how can the general population know what to do?

I first became aware of this while I was studying for my veterinary doctorate at Tufts. But it wasn't until the year after I graduated, when I did my exotic animal rotation at the Animal Medical Center in New York City, that I really began to understand how much we didn't know about caring for these unique animals. People would bring in their pet parrots, turtles, and rabbits, and we vets would struggle just to diagnose their conditions properly. We were often at a total loss as to how to treat them.

Although I'd originally planned on becoming an internist for dogs and cats, during my time at the Animal Medical Center I felt called to specialize in exotics, and it's been my mission for almost two decades now to learn as much as I can about these animals and provide them with the best possible care.

Even a red-eared slider turtle so small that it fits in your back pocket requires a special blend of TLC. In fact, for their size these popular pets require a lot of specialized care. I will never forget Gertie, who had the telltale red stripe on each side of her head, just behind the eyes, that gives sliders their name. She was four years old and had been fed only iceberg lettuce her whole life, because her owners had read that she needed greens. Like most exotic pets, red-eared sliders need to eat a variety of foods to get all the vitamins, minerals, and other nutrients they need. Her owners didn't realize that iceberg lettuce isn't really a green; it's essentially water with almost no nutrients. It's not good for turtles, and it doesn't have much of a nutritional benefit for people, either.

Gertie had never seen a vet before she came to see me, as she had never been sick before. Cat and dog owners generally don't hesitate to seek out veterinary care when their animals get sick, and they also make annual visits for vaccines and wellness exams. But exotic pet owners tend to wait until their animals are very ill before they seek help, which was what Gertie's owners had done. They had realized something was wrong only after her behavior changed, and quite drastically. Whereas most any other animal could not have survived on only lettuce for as long as Gertie did, because she's a reptile with an extremely slow metabolism, she was able to function for longer. For four years she had energetically swum to the end of her tank to greet her owners, Jodie and Bruce, whenever they entered the room, but now she no longer appeared to recognize them. (Despite popular misconception, turtles really do know their owners.) She spent the majority of her days listless in the corner of her tank, unresponsive to her owners' voices. Jodie and Bruce didn't know what to do, and fortunately they sought help. When they arrived at my hospital, I could sense immediately that their fondness for their pet turtle was clearly as great as that of any dog or cat owner. I examined Gertie's top and bottom shells; the carapace and plastron, respectively, as they are called. They were the consistency of a sponge, and I could easily indent her shell by pressing down on it with my index finger. Her head and limbs were limp and hanging out, and she appeared to have no muscle strength left to pull them back in.

I immediately performed a minor surgical procedure to place a red rubber tube through the skin in the side of her neck, through the wall of her esophagus, down into her stomach to feed and medicate her. We put her in the intensive care unit with an ultraviolet lamp shining brightly on her shell to jump-start the production of vitamin D, which is essential both for reptiles and mammals to absorb calcium from their food.

After a few days in the ICU, Gertie began to show positive signs of recovery, and we sent her home, still with the feeding tube sutured to the opening in the skin on her neck in case she needed additional feedings and still couldn't eat on her own. But at least she was alive. I gave Jodie and Bruce detailed written instructions on how to care for Gertie during recovery, including how to feed her liquid food and calcium through the tube if she continued to be unable to eat on her own. Then I said a silent prayer that she would heal.

After I hadn't heard from Bruce or Jodie for several weeks, I sadly concluded that Gertie had succumbed to malnutrition and passed away. But nearly three months later, I got a call that Gertie was moving and eating again on her own. Two weeks after that, they reported that she'd become strong enough to rip out the sutures that kept her tube in place, and she'd pulled out the tube herself. She was once again kicking her way from one end of her tank to the other! Her owners couldn't believe the physical transformation—her squishy shell had hardened once again.

"Thank you, Doctor," Bruce and Jodie said. "We worried she wouldn't make it."

"Spinach, squash, peppers, carrots—even hay," I instructed. "Keep feeding her the good stuff, and she'll stay strong."

They thanked me again and promised, "No more iceberg lettuce."

Bruce and Jodie had never meant to harm Gertie. They'd simply been unaware of what she needed to survive and stay healthy. Like so many owners of exotics, they'd had the right intentions but not enough good information.

But Bob Dixon didn't need a lecture from me on how to care for his beloved sugar gliders. He'd always done everything by the book, and then some, for Lily. A couple of years ago, he'd brought Lily in for a routine checkup and shared with me an article saying that gliders feel more secure eating up high, as they do in their native habitat of old-growth eucalyptus forests. In the wild, sugar gliders hardly ever touch the ground and glide from tree to tree seeking sweet sap and insects.

"I thought I'd build her a wooden nest box atop a series of elevated perches and platforms I'd secure in her cage. Kind of like her own loft or walk-up apartment."

I appreciated Bob's woodworker imagination and added my own entrepreneurial twist. "I think you could make a fortune building and selling glider apartments to other glider owners."

Of all the pet owners who came through my hospital doors, I knew for certain that Bob was doing everything right. If his gliders, Lily and Mathilda, were both gravely sick, something was horribly wrong. Refocusing my attention on the animals, I said, "I'd like to keep them both at the hospital today and possibly overnight to run some blood and chemistry tests and monitor their vitals. Would that be all right with you?"

"I was hoping you'd say that," he said, pausing and shifting from foot to foot. "I don't want my wife to know how sick they are."

Bob had been very clear from his first visit to the hospital years ago that I should not call him at home or mail notes, appointment reminders, or information about Lily's health to his home address. Bob would call me from his private work line whenever he had a question, and he paid for every visit in cash. Whenever he brought Lily in, he parked his Ford F100 behind the hospital and out of view of passing cars on the two-lane main road. Marnie and I joked that it was as if Lily were in a witness-protection program.

Bob's glider had been a patient of the hospital for nearly a year before I had the nerve to ask, "I'm curious . . . why are you so secretive about Lily's care?"

At once, the muscles around his stubbly jawline tensed, and I wished I'd left it alone.

"On second thought," I said, "it's really none of my business."

Bob Dixon wasn't the first pet owner to make special requests. Ana Fieldsworth, for example, who regularly boards her umbrella cockatoo, Althea, at the hospital when she goes on vacation with her husband, isn't shy about asking for favors. As extravagant as her owner, Althea is a large bird with a prominent crest of white feathers on her head and long white tail feathers dusted with yellow. The first time Ana left Althea with us, I asked Ana what we could do to ensure that her parrot would be comfortable while she was away. Typically, owners' requests are fairly straightforward, such as placing a favorite toy in the cage or scratching their animals in a special spot they particularly like, which makes them feel more at home.

"Well, there is one thing," she chirped.

"Absolutely. What is it?"

"On weekends Chase and I enjoy reading the Sunday *Times* with some good bagels and salmon spread."

"Mmmmm," I agreed. "That's a nice ritual." I made a mental note to surprise Peter with a similar spread that Sunday.

"Yes, and Althea loves it, too," Ana said. "Although she prefers her salmon spread on crackers."

I looked at her for a moment until it registered that she was asking me to serve Sunday brunch to Althea.

"Um, okay," I responded with some hesitation. "So you'd like us to get salmon spread for Althea?"

"Oh, God, goodness no," Ana protested. "I'll go to Zabar's to pick it up myself and drop it off before we leave on Friday."

"Zabar's, on the Upper West Side?" Manhattan was a good hour's drive from where Ana lived.

"Yes, that's the one. Are you familiar with them?"

"Of course. Very good food." But that wasn't the point. This was a tall order even for an extravagant bird.

But before I could balk, Ana clapped her hands together and said, "Well then, that settles it. I'll pick some salmon spread up for you, too."

The truth is that every pet owner has his or her own way of doing things, and who am I to question anyone's ritual? In my own home, Peter doesn't wake up until Gizmo, our biggest gray cat, swipes at his forehead with his paw. The feline has become a more effective alarm clock than the digital version that blasts sports commentary before the sun is up.

So after that first awkward inquiry, I had not asked Bob again why he was cagey about Lily's care. But now—five years later—he seemed to be offering an explanation.

"My wife, Jeanne, has never approved," Bob said. "Says Lily is a silly little pet for a big guy like me."

With his calloused hands and somewhat rigid gait, Bob did look like the kind of man you'd expect to see with a Labrador retriever or a German shepherd. But if I'd learned anything from my years of practice, it was that you can't help whom you love. Many of us fall for unlikely companions—and this includes pets too.

"My affection for Lily embarrasses her. *I* embarrass her." He shifted his gaze toward Mathilda. "And then I brought home another one. She went through the roof."

Bob paused, and his words sunk in. The disappointment. The shame. The secrecy. And still—an unyielding devotion to his animals. I finally understood the heart of Bob's conflict. However much his wife loved Bob, only Lily, and now Mathilda, accepted him without terms and conditions.

How many times had I witnessed this? Pets make up for all manner of disappointing human relationships in our lives.

A few years ago, Susan Mitchell brought in her elderly guinea pig, Rosie, with a severe staphylococcus infection. It was one of the worst I'd seen. The charcoal-dipped guinea had scratched herself raw from the skin irritation the bacteria were causing, and she had a rectal prolapse, meaning that portions of her colon were exposed and necrotic. She clearly needed blood work, massive IV antibiotics, and possibly surgery.

"It's bad, isn't it? Is she going to die?" Susan asked as she paced back and forth in the examination room.

"She's in pretty bad shape," I had to agree. "How old is she?"

"I got her for my twelfth birthday when we moved from Buffalo to Manhattan. She was my first pet."

Guinea pigs are common first pets, and I frequently recommend them to parents who aren't sure what to give their child for a first animal. They tend to be friendly, interactive animals, making them great for kids to watch and hold. Generally calm when kids touch them, they even make purring noises, like cats, when they are happy. Their signature squeak makes small children giggle, and when they are excited, young guinea pigs will often jump straight up into the air, a behavior called popcorning. Sometimes, an ill guinea pig is just old, arthritic, and weak. Their average life span is around seven to eight years, but Susan looked to be about twenty-five, which would make Rosie in the neighborhood of thirteen.

"Rosie's been with me through everything—my first kiss, when I started driving, went to prom, and graduated from college. When I got engaged, Rosie was the first to know!"

I looked at Susan sympathetically and thought of my own devoted companion, Dale, a parrot who had likewise taken my side through breakups, makeups, and other life events. Dale was a baby when he "found" me. During my internship, I was at a pet store taking blood for an avian study, and a little green-and-blue squawky parrot kept hopping off his perch to chew on my sleeve. No matter how many times I shooed him away, he continued to hop over and demand my attention. I finally realized he was trying to tell me something: I am yours, and you are mine. I adopted Dale that afternoon and took him home. Twenty years later, Dale lives with me still.

I gently picked up Rosie and examined the dried out, dark-colored colon protruding from her rectum. Rosie's infection had been ignored for some time, which didn't make sense given the shared history together that Susan was describing.

A cell phone buzzed in Susan's pink Kate Spade purse. She quickly pulled it out, checked who it was, and just as abruptly put it away.

"That's my husband, Keith," she said a minute later. "We just made an offer on a house in Connecticut. He's worried about the money. We have car payments, bills, and, well"—her voice trailed off—"he's not really a pet person."

"Shall I let you two speak in private?"

"No." Tears welled up in her eyes. "I don't want to talk to him right now."

I placed Rosie back in Susan's arms. As if she couldn't help it, tears tumbled down her face and onto Rosie's dark coat. I reflexively handed her a tissue.

"Thank you," she whispered.

"Take as much time as you need."

"I love him," she said and swallowed hard, "but Keith doesn't see Rosie the same way I do." She stroked the top of Rosie's head, and the aged guinea pig gently closed her eyes and purred at Susan's touch. "She's my best friend."

"Of course she is," I said.

I've seen firsthand, countless times, how animals can expand and change the lives of the people who take them into their homes. Traditional dog and cat owners may find it hard to imagine that a spiny hedgehog or a squawky macaw can also snuggle and nuzzle and make an affectionate pet or that even the clumsiest potbellied pig can walk on a leash, but

I've witnessed unbreakable bonds between humans and these special animals that defy explanation again and again.

"Would you believe my best friend is a cranky old parrot?" I asked. "Although when I first got him he was just a sweet baby with a newly feathered, fuzzy head."

Susan gave me a weak smile and dabbed at the corners of her eyes. Her diamond solitaire caught the light. Three carats, maybe four—it was hard to miss. She followed my gaze and tucked her hand away.

"Take a minute," I said, "while I consult my head tech on how best to start treating for the treatable." Vets commonly make this statement when a patient is in a fragile state. It means we'll give the best possible treatment we can, but some things may be beyond our power to remedy or heal.

I slipped out of the examination room and found Marnie in the break room, sipping a Diet Coke and snacking on pretzels.

"What's wrong?" she asked with her mouth full. "You look like you're gonna blow."

"I might."

Though I can almost always help my patients, humans are an altogether different animal. "I just need to take a moment and remind myself that I'm a vet, not a marriage counselor," I said.

"Oh, that," Marnie said with matched irritation. "He's not going to let her do it, you know."

I looked at her sideways.

"I heard her on the phone earlier, in the waiting room— pleading with him for the money to treat her. Reminds me of Jim." She rolled her eyes, referring to her ex-husband. "The man wouldn't even buy toilet paper without first checking the monthly budget."

Marnie had often griped about her ex's control of the household finances. It was one reason they'd split.

I sighed. "Well, it's not going to be cheap." I slumped down beside Marnie and popped a few of her pretzels into my mouth. "I don't know when I've seen a guinea pig in worse shape. She desperately needs surgery."

I worried that Marnie was right. In the face of a looming mortgage, I could guess that even if the figure to treat Rosie were nominal, Susan's husband would refuse.

Marnie and I returned to the examination room together just as Susan was getting off her phone. She stood pressed against the back wall, the posture of someone who's accepted defeat.

Marnie and I exchanged a concerned look, and then I said, "Rosie needs extensive repair. I cannot make her better without performing surgery, and this will likely be costly. I'm sorry."

Susan nodded and took in a choked breath. I imagined she was confronting the choice before her: saving Rosie or saving her marriage.

I thought about Susan's dilemma now as I watched Bob's interplay with Lily and Mathilda. He gave Lily another slight tug on her tiny ear and drew in a deep breath. "Lily has been the source of relentless arguments between Jeanne and me over the years. The deal we ultimately made was that I can have whatever kind of pet I want—as long as it doesn't cost us any money." Bob leaned forward in his chair. "But as you and I both know, Dr. Hess, pets cost money."

Yes, they do, I thought. And especially when they're sick.

9:42 A.M.

As I CAME out of the examination room with Lily and Mathilda nestled in my arms, Marnie stopped short in the hallway to look at them. "I'll admit them to the ICU and start them on antibiotics for possible bacterial infection," she said. Marnie often knows what I'm going to say before I say it—the result of working together for over a decade.

"Yes, and run blood tests to check organ function. Catch me up on their status in an hour." As Marnie tore down the hall, I looked at my watch and sighed, realizing that Peter had already gotten the boys off to school and I'd missed them. I made myself a promise to make it home in time for family dinner. Just then, Colette, my associate vet, turned the corner, clipboard in hand, and nearly knocked me over. I'm barely over five feet tall, and she's close to six.

"Time to start rounds, Laurie. Ready to go over the schedule?" Colette was working double duty this week, standing in also for the hospital's receptionist, and I was impressed by how naturally she performed both tasks. She exudes authority, which she uses when addressing the hospital staff, but she can also slip into a sweet maternal role with clients. Perhaps it's because she is a new mother herself, having recently given birth to a baby boy. Her natural warmth was evident when she greeted owners and their pets in the waiting room, creating a calm and welcoming atmosphere that is of paramount importance in making our visitors comfortable. Depending on the day, the hospital could be rife with a multitude of emotions, running the gamut from happiness and relief to grief and despair.

"I'm ready," I said. "Lay it on me."

"First, you'll check in with and prep Sally, a ferret in for a cystotomy later this afternoon. But before the actual removal of the bladder stone, we have appointments stacked every thirty minutes, starting with a lop-eared rabbit that is new to the practice and in for gastrointestinal issues."

"What's the new patient's name?" I asked.

"Peter," she said with a smirk.

"Naturally. Okay, who else?"

"Next we have Chilly, a chinchilla in for a possible foreign body ingestion; a bandage changing for Masey, an umbrella cockatoo with a fractured wing. After that you have a short break before the McNeal family brings in their family of rats for their yearly checkups." Colette added, "Morris, you may remember, is the youngest in the family and an expert escape artist. Watch out for that one."

"Noted," I said, remembering the day a gecko had escaped from my grip and crawled up the wall of the examination room, using the suction cups on the bottom of its feet to cling to the ceiling. There he had stayed until I climbed onto a step stool and coaxed him down the wall with an umbrella handle.

"After that, you have three back-to-back ultrasounds and a short break before the cystotomy surgery."

"And when do we eat lunch?"

That was our joke. Most of the time, the staff ate in short shifts, running from one exam room to the other, stopping along the way to grab a few bites in the lunchroom before running back out. On any given day, our lunchroom looks as though a tornado swept through a convenience store. Cups of yogurt, open bags of chips, and half-eaten sandwiches lie abandoned on the counters and tables.

"Three o'clock as always," Colette said with a wink, "if we're lucky."

Our banter always helps to remind me to keep my spirit light, especially on days like today, with the shadow of Georgie's passing and Lily and Mathilda just admitted to the ICU.

Colette said, "I better get you some more coffee. Half-and-half, no sugar, right?"

"Thanks, Mom," I smiled.

 **4:50 P.M.**

I TOOK FIVE minutes to cram down an egg-salad sandwich and check in with Vets Connect. The postings from earlier in the morning had nearly doubled. I choked on my sandwich. The first one read, "I have a glider in-house right now who is only about 50 grams, seizuring, and non responsive to aggressive supportive care. Any evidence of contagion?" The next post, written by a vet in Massachusetts, read, "Help; sugar gliders sick and unresponsive. If anyone has any diagnostic and treatment suggestions for these guys, I would appreciate hearing about it. I need all the help I can get." This was followed up by a recommendation from another doctor in the tristate area. "I would recommend contacting Dr. Laurie Hess at the Veterinary Center for Birds & Exotics in Bedford. I will cross post your message to the exotic animal board." I froze in my chair. Other veterinarians were seeking *my* help, and while I wanted to offer a treatment plan, my specialized expertise hadn't helped my little patients either. Four gliders placed under my care were now dead, and Lily and Mathilda lay huddled together in a tiny polar fleece blanket in my ICU incubator. Since he'd left them with me that morning, Bob had called me at least a half dozen times to check in, and my report hadn't changed.

"We're syringe feeding them formula so they don't become hypoglycemic, and we're keeping them warm," I told him. "They're lying low in their incubator, and so far, I haven't seen any more seizures."

These were good signs, but I knew that my treatment plan wasn't a solid remedy or a cure. I wasn't treating Lily and Mathilda any differently than I'd treated the others. I was simply buying them time, and I wasn't sure for how long. I suddenly felt the urge to cry, but I willed myself to hold it together. I couldn't add tears to this situation. That wasn't going to help. There had to be a treatment plan that would save Lily and Mathilda—I just didn't know what it was yet.

I logged out of the online group and looked at my schedule. I hadn't made any breakthroughs in the glider case, but I'd somehow juggled an afternoon of back-to-back appointments. I had only one more, and if there weren't any sudden changes in Lily and Mathilda's status, I'd be able to sneak home for dinner with Peter and the boys before returning to the hospital to keep an overnight watch on Lily and Mathilda. Peter would likely be disappointed in my plan to boomerang back to work, but once I shared the news of Georgie's death and Lily and Mathilda's emergency admittance to the hospital, he'd understand. Well, he'd be supportive. My husband freely admits that he's not a science guy and even jokes that the only medicine he knows how to prescribe is children's Tylenol. Peter might not fully understand the severity of Lily and Mathilda's symptoms or the expanding glider crisis, but he would listen to me, which is all I ever really need.

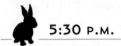

I SWUNG OPEN the examination room door.

"Howdy, Doc!" said a friendly and familiar voice. My extern, Elliot, greeted me with a broad, toothy smile, the kind you expect from a kid who has just had his braces removed. He stood up and extended his hand.

"Come here. I could use a hug, kiddo."

Elliot obliged and leaned in, wrapping an arm around me. He smelled like coffee and snow. Unlike interns, who have already graduated and are fully licensed as veterinarians, veterinary externs like Elliot work at hospitals like mine for a short time while still in school. Elliot had been a first-year veterinary student at Cornell when he enrolled in my summer program. He was already familiar with the hospital because for years I'd routinely cared for his childhood pet, Trixie, a gray-feathered cockatiel with orange-feathered cheeks and a yellow tail. Cockatiels are perhaps the most popular birds kept as pets in the United States. Interactive, friendly, and outgoing, they often love to be handled by or simply hang out with their human "flock mates" (and can even learn to speak a limited vocabulary). Cockatiels also can be silly and playful, bobbing their crest of yellow and gray feathers up and down when they are excited. The right pet brings out our best, brightest self, and that's what I'd seen between Elliot and Trixie. They had drawn out each other's sunniness and playfulness and appeared to know each other intimately.

While Elliot was away at Cornell, he left Trixie at home with his parents. When he returned to Bedford for his summer

externship, he noticed right away from his veterinary training that something was off with his childhood friend. She
sat quietly in her cage, hunched over, her feathers fluffed
up. Birds fluff up their feathers to try to trap warm air
next to their bodies when they are cold or sick. Elliot lec-
tured his parents for positioning Trixie's cage in front of
an air-conditioning vent and moved it to a warmer part of
the house. But after a few days, Trixie's feathers had not
smoothed out, and Elliot knew that she needed more than a
temperature boost.

Birds are a prey species, and when they show any sign of
weakness in the wild, they are hunted and killed. For that reason, they're masters at hiding illness until it's very advanced.
Basically, a bird will mask sickness until it's impossible to hide.
Under my supervision, Elliot ran a series of blood tests on
Trixie and diagnosed his childhood companion with kidney
failure, or gout. This commonly occurs in birds as they age
and is often associated with a lack of essential vitamin A in the
bird's diet (which occurs if they have been eating nothing but
seeds their whole lives). Gout is diagnosed in birds when the
main kidney by-product, uric acid, builds up in their kidneys
and sometimes in their joints, causing painful inflammation.
Elliot asked me to prescribe allopurinol, the drug used to treat
both pets and people with the disease, and he started her on
injections of vitamin A.

Elliot carefully treated Trixie for several weeks in the hospital until it became clear to both of us that she'd become
too sick to treat further or save. When caught early, gout can
sometimes be managed with lifelong medication, but Trixie
no longer had the benefit of time. Gout is progressive and
ultimately fatal for birds.

"Trixie is in pain," he said to me one afternoon as we scrubbed in for a dental surgery on a chinchilla. "I don't want her to suffer anymore, and I'd like to stand in as your technician if you'll let me."

I looked over at him methodically scrubbing, soap dripping down his arms into the surgical sink as he stared ahead. He hadn't explicitly said the words—that he wanted to put Trixie to sleep—but I knew that's what he meant. I said, "Elliot, if you're ready. Of course."

"I am."

I watched him for another moment until I caught his eye. He turned off the faucet and faced me. I said, "Now is when I tell you what I tell every pet owner in this situation—this is the most unselfish thing you can do." I'd said those words many hundreds of times throughout my career, and I meant them wholeheartedly in each instance. "This will be very hard, but it's the right thing for Trixie."

Elliot nodded. "I know that, Dr. Hess. I can do this."

It struck me in that moment that Elliot had the very qualities that my mentor, Dr. Miller, had taught his students to cultivate.

I WAS FIFTEEN years old, standing alone, cold and shivering on the corner of 85th Street and First Avenue in Manhattan, struggling to prevent my knees from buckling under me after finishing my very first day as a high school extern at a local animal hospital. It was the first time I'd seen a dog having surgery. In his tiny surgical suite the size of a closet, Dr. Miller, the veterinarian who would eventually become my chief mentor, had cut into a large liver tumor in a small Westie. In that moment, more blood than I had ever seen exploded all over my scrubs—and the walls—and the floor. The room started to spin, and I was overcome with nausea and terror. Not only did my visceral reaction to the procedure scare me, but I worried that I might throw up in the surgery room. Running for the exit, I pushed open the door with one hand, my other hand clamped over my mouth, willing myself not to vomit. I vaulted through the door and onto the sidewalk, into the bright light, cold air, and loud traffic noise of the city, and I stood there, gasping for breath. Then I backed up to lean against the building, trying not to slide down and end up on the ground. I held my head in my hands, slowly taking in deep breaths.

As the cars sped through the busy intersection, it occurred to me that maybe I couldn't do this, maybe I wasn't strong enough. My long-held dream of becoming a veterinarian started to evaporate.

Just then I felt a firm hand on my shoulder. Dr. Miller had come outside and was standing next to me. I hadn't even noticed he was there.

"You should come inside and watch the rest of the procedure. This dog is going to be okay."

"I can't," I said, swallowing hard and trying to regain some composure. "I thought I could handle this, but I can't."

"Laurie, I want you to look at me. I know the initial shock is hard, but it goes away with time. Most everyone struggles at first, but you learn how to handle it. The best vets handle it with sensitivity, decency, and good, old-fashioned courage."

MY EXTERN, ELLIOT, had all three of these qualities. When he finished his veterinary training at Cornell and sent me news of his acceptance to a paid internship program at a large veterinary hospital in Rhode Island, I was proud of him and honored he'd soon be joining the veterinary community. I sent him a new laptop sleeve with his name stitched on it.

"So, big-time intern," I said, as I sat down across from him now in the examination room, "are you in town visiting your parents for the holidays?"

"Yep, and also"—he paused dramatically and opened his messenger bag—"to bring my new pet back to school with me."

Elliot pulled out a three-foot-long king snake.

He smiled. "Meet Scarlet. Isn't she gorgeous?" The snake curled up in the crook of Elliot's arm, and her tongue darted in and out of her mouth to assess the situation around her. She was strikingly beautiful. Prominent black bands set against vibrant red distinguished her from the venomous coral snake, whose red markings are always married to yellow. *Red on yellow will kill a fellow. Red on black is a friend of Jack.* She began to travel up Elliot's arm, and I could tell by the way she responded to his gentle touch that she felt safe with him. Yet I was bewildered. *Hadn't Elliot always been a bit squeamish around snakes?* Like many veterinary students, Elliot gravitated toward a particular species and class of animal. For him—unsurprisingly, given his relationship with Trixie—it was birds. But as an exotic animal doctor, you're required to handle and treat all classes—feathers, fur, and scales. Not until Elliot was a visiting student at my hospital was he exposed to the wide range of animals I treat on a daily basis, and that was when he had his first real contact with snakes. I remember the first time I asked him to assist me as I examined Henry, a thirty-pound python, for a possible skin infection; Elliot had actually recoiled into

the corner of the examination room. "Come back over here,"
I'd encouraged him. I understood his common misconception
that snakes are slimy and prone to bite. But Henry was neither. "This old guy is absolutely harmless. Look, he even gives
kisses." I lifted Henry up off the examination table, and right
on cue he stuck out his forked tongue and flicked my cheek. (In
actuality, reptiles use their tongues to smell and sample their
chemical environment—this is called tropotaxis—and Henry
was likely getting a whiff of the Paul Mitchell hairspray that
I use liberally to tame my curls, but I think Elliot understood
the point I was trying to make: pet snakes are most often gentle and friendly creatures.) It took several introductions in the
supervised and controlled environment of the hospital to allay
Elliot's fear and allow him to relax. He admitted one day as he
swaddled a bearded dragon that even the "cold-blooded" were
quite cuddly. Still, I had been sure that when he was ready to
adopt another pet, he'd get another cockatiel, much as another client, Rose Adler, had done after she'd lost Charlie, her
parakeet of many years.

Within a week of losing Charlie to old age, Rose had called
me to say that she needed a new bird and would I please help
her find one. I understood that she was devastated and wanted
to fill the emptiness that Charlie had left behind, but I advised
against getting a new pet so soon and suggested that she wait.

"It's important that you allow yourself the time to grieve
and understand that Charlie cannot ever be replaced, even if
you get another bird."

I haven't met a pet owner who didn't suffer great sadness
when a cherished companion became sick or died. And at the
time of their loss, many owners swear to me that they'll never

have another pet. But in time almost all of them change their minds. My reason for this is that pet people are always pet people. Our human longing for companionship and the desire to care for another living being is undeniable and strong. So despite the near inevitability of another loss down the road, most of us animal lovers open our hearts and homes again. Though a new pet will never replace a pet we've lost, welcoming a new companion into our lives helps to ease our grief so that we can eventually heal and love again.

Rose, however, didn't want to wait or ease into anything. It seemed that she wanted to skip over the grieving process altogether. She called me every couple of days, insisting she was ready to get another bird. Finally, I gave in and agreed to help her. I knew of someone who rescued Quaker parrots.

"But I don't want a *parrot*," Rose said, with what sounded like a little disdain.

"Quaker parrots are quite similar to parakeets," I said. "And they're friendly, bond to their owners, can learn tricks, live a long time, they're smart, and like parakeets, they're a little squawky. But a Quaker parrot is different enough that you will feel as if you are adopting a new bird. Remember, no bird will ever be exactly like Charlie. Every animal has its own distinct personality and traits that you grow to know and love over time."

I looked at Elliot now, in his thick, horn-rimmed glasses that fall down his nose, with a red-and-black-striped snake looped around his arm. No doubt, Scarlet couldn't be more different, in appearance anyway, from his childhood bird, with her tangerine cheeks and lyrical song. I wondered if this was Elliot's unique way of recovering from his loss and moving on.

THE LAST TIME I'd seen the markings of a king snake in the hospital, they had encircled the wrist of another extern in the bold black and red ink of a tattoo. Jackson, another visiting vet student, was in the same summer program as Elliot. On his first day, he stomped through the hospital halls in his motorcycle boots, acting as if he were already a doctor to whom my technicians should answer. His attitude was bossy, overly opinionated, and contradictory. I sensed right away that he might not be easy to work alongside, even for a short period. Still, I'd been willing to give him a chance.

But in the wake of Trixie's passing, his callousness toward Elliot showed me that he did not have the critical qualities I deem necessary to make a good veterinarian.

I'd heard them loading up on coffee one afternoon when I was getting some gauze out of the supply closet across from the break room.

"Bro, you definitely need some caffeine," Jackson said.

"What do you mean?"

"What do I *mean*?" Jackson said with exaggeration. "It's like—where's Elliot? We're assisting Dr. Hess on surgery today, and your head is totally somewhere else. I know you lost your pet, but you need to seriously ask yourself whether you're cut out to do this if you're going to break down every time an animal dies."

My mouth fell open. Elliot walked swiftly out of the break room and caught me standing in the hallway, frozen in place.

"I'm sorry," I mouthed the words. He lowered his head and continued down the hall.

I wanted to strangle Jackson for attacking Elliot, who, in my opinion, was mourning his childhood companion just as he should—like a human being. Instead, I looked around for

Marnie. I found her in the nearest exam room, patiently clipping a ferret's nails.

"I cannot believe him!" I sputtered.

"What are you talking about?" she asked calmly and clipped a nail.

"Jackson! He has no sensitivity. He just said the most hurtful thing to Elliot who is the *most* sensitive. Jackson could learn a thing or two about bedside manners from Elliot."

She sighed. "Let him go."

"You mean, let 'it' go or dismiss him from the program?" I'd never done that before. *But maybe Marnie was right.* The type of extern and future doctor I wanted to help cultivate is kind to every animal he treats, regardless of species, and empathetic to the emotions of clients who may be very emotional over the illness or death of their pets. I also only wanted students who were team players. Jackson, so far, hadn't exhibited any of these characteristics. Without them, I don't believe an individual can be successful in this profession.

Marnie clipped another nail and looked up at me. "What do you think is best for the hospital? What do you think is best for him?" Whereas I was reacting to the situation emotionally and in defense of Elliot, Marnie was taking her characteristic mature approach.

I said, "Perhaps it is better for Jackson to realize now, early on, what he needs to change and decide if this is the right career path to follow."

Marnie nodded her approval and went back to her work.

Jackson was in my program for another two days before I asked him to leave. When I suggested he might find another veterinary hospital in which to complete his externship, he just nodded, picked up his leather jacket, and walked out.

This final demonstration of detachment and insensitivity confirmed for me my decision to let him go. He was not the right
fit for my hospital.

I RETURNED MY focus to Elliot as he curled Scarlet's tail
around his wrist. "It's great to see you again." I winked. "You
always warm up the room. And I'm glad you've found a new
pet. Any animal is lucky to have you."

8:30 P.M., HOME

FINALLY IN MY driveway, I slid out of the car and looked up
at the sky. It was clear, brilliant, and cold. I cinched my jacket
in close and turned toward the warm glow of light pouring
out from our large, picture-frame kitchen window. Through
it, I could see long and lanky Brett, my studious eighth grader,
bent over a stack of books at our long pine kitchen table. In
the next room, I suspected, his younger and more relaxed ten-
year-old brother, Luke, and Peter were sprawled out on the
couch, laughing at something on TV. Dale, our cranky pionus
parrot, would be perched on Peter's shoulder, as he often is,
no doubt inserting himself into the conversation with snorts
and chatty squawks. I delighted in envisioning the familiar,
animated scene and trudged toward the house.

I came in with a bang, dragging my purse, gym duffel, and
computer bag into the kitchen. All four cats swarmed around
my feet, meowing loudly for me to feed them. Dale screamed
a loud "Hello baby" from the den, and Lennon and Ringo,
Luke's singing canaries, joined in the call of the wild from
their cages upstairs.

"How's it going, honey?" I said to Brett as I walked over to where he was doing his homework among a pile of crumpled papers and empty snack wrappers.

"Hi, Mom," he mumbled as he slipped off his headphones. "Did you bring dessert?"

A typical welcome home. As much as I'd hoped to make it to the table for dinner, I was arriving late, in time only for dessert. This was no big surprise. Peter was accustomed to my long and late hours, and on the rare occasions when I did make it through the back door before the dinner dishes were cleared, he'd tease, "Doc, you feeling okay?" Brett and Luke equally enjoy ribbing me. They've even nicknamed me "Dessert Lady," not just because I'm often late getting home but also because I guiltily bring them dessert.

"Salted caramel pie," I whispered in his ear.

His eyes widened. "Don't tell Luke. I want to cut the first piece."

Even though Peter and the boys have gotten used to the routine, every time I'm late I regret it. If I were a better mom, I think as I mentally kick myself, I'd be home every night in time to *make* dinner. But since opening the animal hospital, I've become more reliable with whipped cream.

2

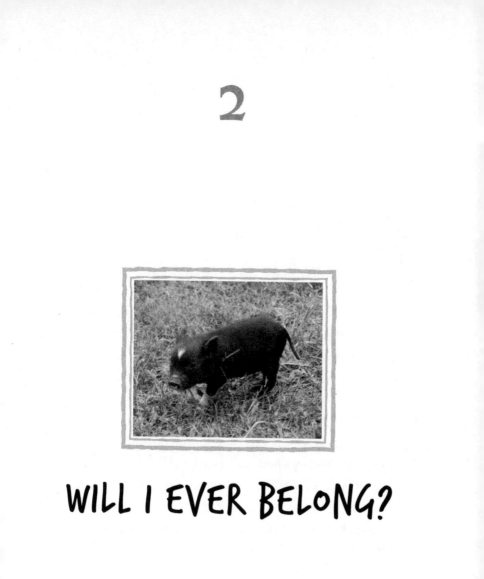

WILL I EVER BELONG?

TUESDAY, 7:00 A.M., HOME

As I backed out of our driveway into the icy street,
I nearly hit my neighbor Katherine's recycle bin, perfectly
stacked with aluminum cans and neatly folded cardboard
boxes.

"Crap," I said out loud. "Is it garbage day?" I glanced back
toward the garage where our two full bins stood, crammed full
of loose paper and crushed soda bottles. It was Brett and Luke's
responsibility to haul them down to the street every week, but
since neither Peter nor I could ever remember when collection day was, how could we blame the boys for also forget-
ting? When we moved to Mount Kisco from New York City,
we went nearly three weeks waiting for a garbage pickup that
never came. When I finally called the city and complained, an
accommodating and bemused woman told me that garbage
pickup "doesn't just happen out here." She explained that every homeowner must arrange for pickup. After years of living
in city apartments, Peter and I had also assumed that TV cable
service would be almost automatic. In the city, when you want

to install cable, you simply call someone and say, "Turn it on." But in our new neck of the woods upstate, homes don't come prewired for HBO.

I put the car into park, jumped out, and marched up the long driveway to drag the containers across our gravel driveway. The pebbles crunched under my boots as I rolled the bins down to the street, and I glanced up at Katherine's front window, half expecting to see her tight ponytail and customary frown, but the curtains were still pulled shut. I hopped back into the warmth of the car and tore off down the street.

The night before, Katherine had caught me arriving home late—for the second time. After I had helped Brett put the finishing touches on his PowerPoint presentation for school and both boys had gone off bed, I'd returned to the hospital to keep a late-night watch on Lily and Mathilda. When I finally lumbered home, it was after 2 a.m., so it was actually morning. From inside the dark car I noticed Katherine in a pink chenille robe, slowly pacing around her spacious white kitchen with Amelia, her newborn, curled over her shoulder. At this hour, I thought, she was probably up heating a bottle or attempting to lull a fussy baby back to sleep. She noticed my headlights and went to the window to glare across the moonlit lawn in my direction. Katherine had been overtly critical of me and my "frequent absences from home" since the day we had moved in across the street. She was constantly gossiping about me with other neighbors, who dutifully reported back to me.

At last year's neighborhood holiday party, after I'd had a rum-spiced cider, I overheard her snicker and say to another guest, "She's always at that zoo. I don't know who's raising those boys."

Peter heard it, too, and calmly led me out of the room before I could respond. "Ignore her," he whispered, gently squeezing my arm. "She doesn't know what she's talking about."

"It's an animal hospital," I said quietly, fuming.

He squeezed my arm a little tighter and smiled. "It's not going to kill you to get along."

"It might."

If her son Gilman and our son Brett hadn't been classmates from an early age and now playing on the same soccer team, I'd happily have told Katherine to mind her own business. But it did make more sense to try to get along. At least, that's what Peter said.

In the sixteen years since we'd moved from Manhattan to Westchester County, I'd found that the acceptable roles for women in my area were about as current as black-and-white television. You'd never guess we were only an hour's commuter train ride outside Manhattan, where professional women abound. But in our suburban town, most women stay home.

Peter and I had wrestled over the decision to move here. We'd both grown up in the city and loved its high energy and pace and the accessibility it offered to all things educational and entertaining. Still, when the time came to start a family, we knew we both wanted a different experience for our children—principally, a yard to play in and more than one bathroom to share. When I finished my residency at the Animal Medical Center in Manhattan, we moved out of our high-rise on East 86th Street and bought a 1750 saltbox colonial in Mount Kisco. With 3,000 square feet inside and two acres in the back, which Peter's parents, natives of Brooklyn, referred to as "the grounds," it more than fulfilled our fantasy of spacious country living. We'd made the right decision to move;

Peter and I were both confident about that. Yet, nearly two decades later, something still felt a little bit off. Mount Kisco had most certainly become home, but Katherine's sneering comments helped to reinforce my feeling that I didn't really belong here. Would I ever?

THE NIGHT BEFORE I had driven down Route 117, blessedly free of traffic at ten-thirty at night, and pulled into the hospital parking lot in just over five minutes. I'd found Lily and Mathilda both lying flat on their cage floor, stretched out, eyes closed. They were clearly weak; any healthy glider would have been active and curious at this time of night and climbing the walls of his or her cage. Still, I was relieved that their status was no worse than a few hours before. It seemed I'd bought myself some more time.

I retreated to my dark office, determined to spend some uninterrupted, quiet time poring over veterinary journals. I thought there must be a published paper that could explain the gliders' symptoms—weakness, lack of appetite, trembling. I flipped through the *Journal of Exotic Pet Medicine* and sifted through my stack of zoo and wildlife textbooks, but many hours later I hadn't found a single written report that went beyond naming nutritional deficiency as the cause of the symptoms. And I'd already ruled that out.

I turned back to my computer and opened a new browser window. I typed in "sugar gliders for sale" and "Johnson Valley Mall." Bob had said he'd bought Lily at a mall, and Johnson Valley was one of the biggest in the area. I hit enter, and immediately up popped a story posted on Westchesterjournal. com. The headline read, "Perfect-Sized Pockets of Fun Briefly

Sold at Johnson Valley Mall." I followed the link and scanned the story: "Sales on appliances and electronics aren't the only thing drawing shoppers' attention at Johnson Valley. For a limited time, Sugar Buddies has set up shop in the Central Court selling an animal called a sugar glider. The animals cost $500 for a total kit, which includes instructions on how to care for them, a new cage and a month's supply of food. For four days, shoppers can stop for a demonstration of these small, gliding marsupials in the same general family as a kangaroo or koala bear."

I stared at the accompanying photo of a baby glider with a tiny bubble gum pink nose and matching feet poised to leap into the air. Bob hadn't remembered the name of the vendor he'd adopted Mathilda from, but this had to be the one. I scrolled down the page. "Sugar Buddies has been selling exotic animals at malls throughout the tri-state area." Hadn't Maxine also purchased Georgie from a mall in upstate Connecticut?

PETER'S READING LIGHT was still on when I slid into bed. He was fast asleep, propped up by pillows, the TV remote control in one hand and *Sports Illustrated* in the other. I folded up the magazine and glanced at the clock—2:32 a.m., much later than I'd intended to get home.

"Peter," I whispered.

He cracked open a sleepy eye and squinted at the clock. "Home before breakfast? I wasn't expecting you until coffee time."

"Very funny," I said and turned off his light. "I think I'm onto something."

He pulled back the covers. "Well, then, get into bed and tell me about it before it's time to get up."

I crawled into bed and unraveled what I'd discovered about Sugar Buddies while Peter listened quietly and attentively.

"What if Bob and Maxine's gliders are somehow linked?" I finally concluded. "The article said the company is selling exotic animals at malls throughout New York, New Jersey, and Connecticut."

"It sounds plausible," he said into the darkness. "Let's see what I can dig up." He reached over and turned back on his reading light, fumbling for his glasses.

My husband the lawyer welcomes every opportunity he can to play detective. I've always teased him that criminal defense, not entertainment law, is his true calling.

Our mutual friend Marjorie set us up when Peter was studying at Harvard Law and I was in veterinary school at Tufts. Marjorie had somehow convinced herself, as she tried separately to convince us, that we'd be "perfect together," I guess since we are both native New Yorkers on the bookish, nerdy side. At her insistence, we agreed to meet at an Italian restaurant in the North End of Boston.

From the moment we sat down, I began rattling on, as I tend to do when I'm nervous, about my senior year of clinical rotation when I suddenly realized we'd gotten through the entire first course and Peter had hardly said a word. Or, more accurately, I hadn't given him the opportunity to say much of anything. I put down my fork, took a deep breath, and said, "I talk a lot. I'm sorry. Enough about me. I want to know about you."

"Okay. What do you want to know?" he said. I liked that he smiled easily.

"Let's see, tell me about your family, like what does your father do?"

Peter cleared his throat and shifted uncomfortably in his chair. He took a sip of his pinot.

Oh, good going, Laurie. His father must be dead.

"Peter, I'm sorry. Is he—?"

"He's a furrier." Peter set down his glass.

"Oh!" I said with surprise. *The fur trade?* I hadn't seen that coming.

"And something tells me you wouldn't be interested in a mink coat at a great discount?"

Peter's smile returned, and I couldn't help but smile back. Underneath the guise of a Harvard-educated attorney, he was playful, and when he recognized that I also had a sense of humor (when I didn't throw red paint on him and storm out of the restaurant in protest), we relaxed. The second course was animated and flirtatious. It didn't hit another sour note until he told me he'd never had a pet growing up.

"Not even a bird?" I said, astonished.

"Especially not birds," he said.

My mouth fell open. "Are you serious? You do realize my specialized area of study is avian medicine?"

He took a sip of wine. "That's birds, right?"

"Yes." I nodded, amused. "That's right."

"Yeah," he shook his head. "Birds are definitely the worst."

He was baiting me, and I couldn't resist. "Really? How so?" I asked.

"I grew up in Brooklyn, and you know, birds are everywhere. One of my more haunting childhood memories is getting caught in a flock of pigeons as they're swooping and swarming all around me." Peter swatted at the air, ducking in mock horror.

"Wow, that does sound horrible," I said, teasing.

Actually, the fact that he hadn't had a pet really did upset me. I'm always saddened when I hear that a child doesn't have a pet. As far as I'm concerned, pets and kids go together like ice cream and a hot summer day. I thought back to our family bird, Chips, a gray-cheeked parakeet who lived in a cage that hung from the ceiling in our dining room throughout my childhood, and of my grandmother's beloved blue budgies. Their names all began with the letter *p*—Petey, Popo, and Paulie—and their chirps and chatter were the background noise of my upbringing. I couldn't imagine my childhood without any of these feathered friends. And furthermore, I couldn't remember back to a time when I didn't have a pet to love.

"What if I could change your mind about birds?" I said to Peter.

"Changing my mind about birds will require great persuasion."

I leaned forward, looked directly into his eyes, and asked, "Do you have plans after dinner?"

If I'd led Peter to believe that I was taking him home to bed, he didn't give away his disappointment when I asked the taxi to pull up to an after-hours pet store in the Back Bay of Boston.

"It's called immersion therapy," I said as we slid out of the car. I linked my arm through his and led him into the store. "I'm going to desensitize you to birds, so you can get over your phobia. I'll place several different-sized birds on your body. I want you to stand still, if you can."

Peter regarded me dubiously.

"I'll be right here the whole time, don't worry."

"And then what happens?"

"Nothing. That's the whole point of the exercise—you will see that in the presence of birds, nothing bad happens to you. You're safe and okay."

Ten minutes later, Peter was standing frozen in place as a parakeet rested on his forearm, an African gray parrot perched on his shoulder, and a blue-and-gold macaw sat atop his head. He looked like the Christopher Columbus statue in Central Park, one of the more popular roosting places for pigeons.

"How do you feel?" I asked.

"Pretty silly. But relatively calm. When do I get to put my arms down?"

I fumbled in my purse for my point-and-shoot (yes, our first date took place before we had camera phones). "Stand still for one more minute. I want to document this."

I had that photo of Peter tacked above my desk at the hospital for many years to remind me that if Peter can conquer his fears, I, too, can persevere on particularly challenging days.

PETER SAT UP in bed, tapping away on his iPad, as I slathered lotion on my hands. After repeatedly scrubbing them and putting on and taking off sterile gloves all day long, my hands look as though I share DNA with my reptile patients.

"So, super sleuth," I interrupted, "what have you discovered?"

"Not much more than you already have." He took off his glasses and rubbed his temples. "I tend to agree with you that Bob and Maxine's gliders are probably linked to this vendor, Sugar Buddies, but then how do you explain the sickness spreading outside the tristate area?"

I'd been wondering that too. "I don't know, but right now it's the only lead I have."

7:12 A.M., STARBUCKS ON MAPLE AVENUE

I PULLED INTO the drive-through. Peter had sent me off with a travel mug of coffee, but with less than four hours of sleep, I needed something stronger.

"Good morning, Dr. Hess. Your regular double skim cappuccino?" Kelsie Goodwin delivered this as a statement rather than a question. I nodded, admiring her pluck as well as her turquoise nails. She punched in my order and asked, "Anything else?"

"What's the color of that nail polish?" I asked. I like manicured nails, but they were an indulgence I could rarely give myself. What was the point? I'd tried acrylic nails once, when Peter and I had attended a wedding out on Long Island. They'd felt appropriate for the event, but I'd ended up clipping them off a day later, because they got in the way and made it too hard for me to handle the animals at the hospital. I'd regretfully come to the conclusion that my nails need to be clipped short. It's not a glamorous look, but, hey, it's what works for me.

"Don't you love it? It's called 'Naughty Nautical.' I painted Mr. Piggy's toes with it too. He looks amazing."

Mr. Piggy was Kelsie's potbellied pig, who had been my patient since his first annual checkup. The day I met them, I was passing through the waiting room of the hospital as a young woman in a prim, pale yellow, 1950s eyelet dress and black combat boots was pushing a stroller through the front door.

"And who is this little one?" Colette asked, peering over the receptionist's desk.

"Mr. Piggy," the young woman said in an adoring tone.

Exotic pet owners vary widely in age, socioeconomic and marital status, gender, and just about everything else. I've been interviewed many times about my profession, and when I get asked questions such as "What kind of person wants a potbellied pig for a pet?" I typically respond, "It could be anyone. Exotic animals are loved by all types. I really can't generalize."

"Can I see the baby?" I strolled over to sneak a peek. A potbellied pig wearing a baby bonnet stared up at me. (Yes, a baby bonnet. You'd be surprised by how many exotics have their own wardrobes.)

"Isn't he adorable?" she cooed. The black-and-white-spotted pig snorted.

I had to admit, he was pretty darn cute, with his long eyelashes and tiny, pointed, upright ears. I have a weakness for the little ones, and I guessed that Mr. Piggy was still an infant because he looked to weigh less than five pounds. Of course, that would soon change. I wondered if Kelsie knew what she was in for. To say that Mr. Piggy might go through a growth spurt would be an understatement—a growth surge would be more like it. A few months from now, Mr. Piggy would likely outgrow his stroller and become too heavy to carry, at least not without putting quite a strain on Kelsie's lower back.

Though most pigs are small at birth, they often surprise their owners when they quickly grow from little piglets into huge hogs. Even tiny teacup pigs, which start out as small as frosted cupcakes, can plump up into fifty-pound adults. The Vietnamese potbellied pig can reach a hundred pounds or more. This is especially a problem in dense cities such as Manhattan. When a pet pig quickly outgrows the average studio apartment, many owners, not having anticipated how big the animal would get, give them up. Some even abandon them.

Bacon, with his pale-pink skin and sparse raven coat, was one of the first miniature pigs I'd treated after I'd graduated from veterinary school and begun my internship at the Animal Medical Center in Manhattan. His owners, Grant and Meghan, brought him in as a new piglet for routine vaccines and a nail clipping. Such a cute little guy—pink and fuzzy and all of eight pounds—but by the time he was five months old and ready to be neutered, he had ballooned to two hundred pounds. Like other full-sized pigs, Bacon needed to be able to run outside and dig in the dirt. Instead, he was running into the walls and digging into the floors of his owners' second-story brownstone apartment. Getting Bacon down the narrow stairs for a regular walk outside had become a major ordeal for the young couple. They were overwhelmed and didn't know what to do with their little "piggy," who had become as big as a boar.

"If you don't feel you can keep him, I recommend a California sanctuary for abandoned pigs called Lil' Orphan Hammies that might take him," I told them. Bacon's owners contacted the group, and the last I heard, Bacon was living a healthy life outdoors on the sunny West Coast.

Franky was another pig I cared for and treated who had grown from a petite piglet into a 170-pound sow. But whereas Bacon's owners decided they were not able to care for an animal that large, Franky's owner, Rebecca, was determined to maintain a cozy home for the two of them. Also, because she had a rent-controlled apartment on Manhattan's Upper West Side, she wasn't about to move.

So Rebecca managed to pen off an area inside her bedroom for Franky and her favorite blanket, chew toys, and even a small bathing pool. She soundproofed the apartment with panels of foam so that her neighbors wouldn't hear Franky's grunts, snorts, and shrieks, and she paid a couple of neighborhood kids to routinely walk her 170-pound sow down the stairs and around the block for exercise and pee breaks. In the dead of winter, when it was just too cold for the sparsely haired pig to go outside without risking frostbite on her ears and tail, Rebecca trained her to relieve herself on wee-wee pads in the apartment, and for daily exercise she rolled balls around the house for her to chase. Cohabitating with a pig wasn't easy, but for Rebecca it was a labor of love, and she made it work.

The last time I'd seen Rebecca, she'd made the long drive from Manhattan to Westchester with Franky in the back of her Suburban. She was concerned that Franky was scratching at her eyes and blinking often. I suspected she'd developed ulcers on her corneas, which happens commonly in mini pigs. The first challenge to treating Franky was getting her into an examination room. It was a tight squeeze, and once in, she was none too happy about it. She began to stomp around the room, pounding her hoofs into the tile and squealing loudly. When they're throwing a tantrum, pigs behave very much like toddlers; they shriek as though they're being clobbered when they're just objecting to not getting their way.

"Hold her right there!" I shouted to Marnie over Franky's squealing and snorting.

"Got her!" Marnie held Franky's head so that I could check her eyes. To determine her condition and what kind of treatment she might need, I had to spray fluorescein dye directly into her eyes. But every time I got close enough to her pig face to administer the dye, she'd shake her head from side to side and shriek.

"Franky," I said calmly, with my hands on my hips, as if I could reason with her.

She snorted and threw her head back, letting out another screech.

"I need you to sit still. It's almost over." I looked over at Marnie. "On the count of three. One . . . two . . . three."

On my cue, Marnie got hold of Franky's head again and pulled back her eyelids. In one fluid movement I sprayed a droplet of dye onto each of her eyeballs and shined a light into them. As the spray's bright reddish-orange color spread out over the surface of her eyes, I could see small ulcers in the centers of both corneas. Untreated corneal ulcers will eventually cause blindness, but since Franky's ulcers weren't yet that deep, I decided to treat her conservatively with a lubricating eye ointment and antibiotics to soothe her corneas and protect them from additional irritation.

Nearly an hour later, I opened the door of the examination room. The waiting room was packed with pets and their owners waiting to see me, and I felt I needed to explain the noise and the delay.

"My apologies, everyone. You probably heard Franky . . . just throwing a big pig fit," I said with an apologetic smile.

Nobody moved or said a word. Rather, the waiting room seemed frozen in place. All eyes stared at me.

Pete Ferguson, a retired professor, clutched his ailing leopard gecko close to his heart monitor and swallowed hard. Even Dorothy Dunham's pair of chattering parakeets stopped talking to each other. The room was silent save for the sound of traffic from the Saw Mill River Parkway beyond the front door.

What was wrong? Did I have something on my face? Mustard from my turkey sandwich earlier? As I lifted my hand to rub my mouth, I noticed that it was red. The dye! The fluorescein I had used to look at Franky's corneas was splattered all over my lab coat. If you didn't know any better, it could easily be mistaken for blood, and it was all over my hands. No wonder everyone looked stunned.

Pete stood up slowly and backed away from me toward the front door.

"No, no, no, it's not what it looks like." I held up both hands in surrender. "It's just dye."

As another owner stood up to follow Pete's lead, Franky let out a low, contented grunt from the examination room.

"You see?" I said with wild conviction. "She's alive! She's alive!"

FRANKY WAS THE last miniature pig I'd treated at the hospital until Mr. Piggy came along. Baby animals are always a welcome relief from the problems that older and much larger animals need help with. Mr. Piggy was happily snorting and wiggling around in Kelsie's arms.

I took the piglet and set him down on the stainless steel examination table. He was a sweet little guy with a tightly curled tail and a scarlet snout. He squirmed on the cool table, and I asked, "Can I use his blanket to wrap him up."

Kelsie smiled and handed me a thin blue blanket with tiny pigs on it. There was no doubt, Kelsie was a proud pig mama. "Stay still," she gently told Mr. Piggy, "and let the doctor take a good look at you."

I took my penlight out to look into Mr. Piggy's eyes and mouth, as Marnie tried to contain his wriggly little body within the blanket. I then listened to his rapidly beating heart with the same small stethoscope that physicians use to examine human infants. Mr. Piggy was in excellent health after Kelsie's devoted care. His hooves were shiny and trim, and his skin was healthy and smooth.

"He's so clean and well manicured," I said as I inspected his nails.

"I bathe him regularly."

"Really? Most pigs this size don't like to be bathed."

"Mr. Piggy's special."

"What are you feeding him?"

She waved a disciplining finger at Mr. Piggy, who no doubt had a healthy appetite. "He's on a strict pelleted diet with a small amount of vegetables." That explained his smooth, clean skin. Like people, pigs that don't eat a healthful diet have skin problems and tend to develop greasy, flaky coats, even when they're as young as Mr. Piggy.

"Plus I use a manna ball."

These plastic balls have a small opening designed so that food falls out only when a pig pushes or rolls them around, and this activity helps to keep pigs busy. Even tiny teacup pigs like to spend the bulk of their days foraging and rooting around for food. Without exercise, they tend to eat more than they should, so a toy like the manna ball keeps even teacup pigs from rooting around and digging holes in floors and from getting fat and bored.

"Very good," I said.

"I also walk him around my neighborhood park," Kelsie added. "On a leash, of course."

Kelsie had clearly read all the pig-parenting handbooks. I was impressed. When I meet young people like Kelsie with exotic pets, I often worry that they've only gotten the pet for attention or in order to mimic celebrities who have a similar animal, like having the latest designer handbag or trendy hairstyle. But with Kelsie, it was clear she loved Mr. Piggy genuinely.

"You're pretty good at taking care of animals," I said, raising an eyebrow. "Ever thought about becoming a vet?"

"Not a vet, but a pet designer. I'd like to create my own line—a clothing collection for pets," she said suddenly excited. "I'm so into embroidery and appliqué."

With her renegade curls and unapologetic conviction, Kelsie reminded me of myself at her age. She knew who she wanted to be. When I was fifteen and a junior in high school, I did what all my other classmates did and started applying to colleges, except that whereas the majority of the other teens were planning to enter undergraduate programs in business, law, or political science, I decided to pursue veterinary medicine. When I met with my school counselor at the private high school I attended, however, he scoffed at my career choice.

"The students that graduate from *this* high school who want to work in medicine go on to become physicians," he said. "I don't meet many students who want to work with . . . animals." He regarded me with skepticism. "What do your parents say about your 'aspirations'?"

My parents were all for it. They'd always encouraged me to follow my dreams, no matter how untraditional they were. And my interest in animal medicine came as no surprise to them, probably because they were animal lovers themselves. Our eighth-story apartment in Manhattan was home to a menagerie of adopted pets, including dogs, cats, guinea pigs, rabbits, and frogs. We also had an aquarium full of goldfish along with more exotic tropical fish. My father, a prominent New York City attorney, easily confesses that he'd really rather be a farmer.

Throughout my childhood and well into my teen years, my favorite family vacations were the weekend trips to our house on Lake Ashmere in the Berkshire Mountains, home to all kinds of reptiles and amphibians, as well as birds and many other kinds of wildlife. There my fascination with exotic animals blossomed and grew. I spent many solitary hours by the lake, observing the natural environment and all the creatures that lived in it. I developed a deep respect for their special habitat and needs and wondered how I could help protect them both in nature and in captivity.

Despite my high school counselor's disfavor, I followed my own path to vet school, where I sat riveted by lectures on animal curiosities and anomalies, like how penguins keep their feet warm on the ice (they have a special network of blood vessels that circulate heat), how lizards can regrow their tails, and how fuzzy chinchillas release huge clumps of fur—the so-called fur slip—when caught in the mouths of their predators. I loved vet school, as I had known I would, and later in my studies I had my own James Herriot moment when I proudly delivered a baby lamb in the middle of an ice-cold field in early spring. With my team partners cheering me on, I had no doubt that I'd found my tribe—human and animal.

I SMILED AT Kelsie as she handed me my cappuccino.

"Give Mr. Piggy a kiss for me."

She puckered her lips and kissed the air. "Say 'hey' to all the animals at the hospital for me."

With coffee in hand, I zoomed out of the driveway and onto Sunnyslope, toward the hospital.

7:30 A.M., ANIMAL HOSPITAL

I WAS THE first to arrive, so I unlocked the door and re-locked it behind me. I'd learned the hard way that no matter what the hour, if I leave the door open, someone with an animal will come through it. I turned on the lights and computer monitors and rolled up the shades to allow the early-morning sunlight to stream in through the floor-to-ceiling windows.

Right on cue, Target, the hospital's resident African gray parrot, opened an eye and greeted me. "Helloooo."

"Hello, old girl."

Not wanting to miss out on attention, Stop, the female red Eclectus parrot who shares the same cage, came alive with a squawk and a screech.

"Good morning to you, too. I know it's early. I'm not too happy about it either." The two birds splashed around in their water bowls for a few seconds and then started their regular morning exchange.

"RINNNNG . . . RINNNNG . . . ," said Stop.

"HELLOOOOO?" replied Target.

"RINNNNG . . ."

"HELLOOOOO?"

The routine was as established as Target's permanence at the hospital. Everyone knew Target—the staff, patients, and clients alike. She was a fixture in the waiting room, nearly as familiar as

Marnie and Colette. I could hardly remember when she hadn't been part of the team.

Several years before, I had answered a weekend call from local police. "We've apprehended a bird flying around the Target store in Mount Kisco. We think it's a parrot. We need to transport him to your animal hospital for possible identification and treatment."

Apprehended? I'd treated birds that had flown into all manner of windows and gotten entangled in toys. I'd even resuscitated a parrot after his owner rolled over onto him in the middle of the night (like I said, it's not just cats and dogs that love to snuggle and cuddle), but treating a bird that had been arrested—this was new.

"Okay, Officer, I'll be right there."

I arrived at the hospital at the same time that a police car with its siren howling pulled into the parking lot. I walked across and approached a car with two officers squabbling in the front seat.

"You can't just open the door. It'll fly out!" the officer behind the wheel warned.

"Well, I'm not putting my hand back there," his partner asserted. "He already snapped at me once, tried to take my finger off. You've seen that movie, haven't you? Hitchcock, the one with the birds?"

"Uh, yeah, Einstein, it's called *The Birds*. And it's a movie, it's not real."

I would have enjoyed watching the two officers quibble if not for the tiny, frightened bird perched on the headrest in the backseat. I cleared my throat.

"Officers, excuse me. I'm Dr. Hess. You called me about the parrot."

They both whipped their heads around in my direction and then looked back at each other. "She can get him out," they said in unison.

"It's back there," they said, pointing nervously toward the backseat of the squad car.

As they prattled on, warning me about the dangers of trapping a "wild bird," I slipped into the backseat. The parrot was not wild. I know immediately if a bird is wild-caught because around one ankle it wears a metal, ring-like band with an open slit on it, indicating it was put on after the bird was full-grown. Captive-bred birds, like the one I was looking at now, wear a solid metal ring around one ankle that is slipped over the foot when the bird is a baby. At first glance, this bird wasn't much more than maybe four months old, and she was only about five inches tall. She had the typical slate gray feathers of a Congo African gray parrot with a few bright red feathers under her tail. White skin encircled her dark black eyes and her beak. I was pretty sure she was a baby girl.

"Hello, there," I said. "I'm going to get you out of here, okay?" I slowly reached toward her.

"Don't you need a cage, Doctor?" asked one officer. "Or a net?" asked the other.

I ignored their attempts to be helpful and continued to reach my hand out toward the bird. I held my palm open and waited. The baby bird stepped gently onto my finger, and I stroked the top of her head and back.

"You've had quite a rough morning, haven't you?" The bird closed her eyes and relaxed under my touch.

"Well, look at that, he likes you," said the lead officer.

"Actually," I said, "he might be a she."

Indeed, she was a tiny African gray parrot, and she was missing a toe. After a thorough examination, I determined that her injury was well healed, so further treatment wasn't needed. She was a sweet little bird, very tame and so young—the kind of pet parrot owners are dying to have and devastated to lose. How had she gotten lost? I wondered. How had she found her way into Target, and what would happen to her now? I took her back to the hospital with me to look after until we could find her owners.

Colette contacted the local SPCA, and we entered a description of her, mentioning her missing toe, on several lost-and-found national websites such as PetAmberAlert; we even hung a poster in the hospital waiting room: "Lost and Found African Gray Parrot." I was sure someone would claim her; African grays are worth a lot of money, even when missing a toe. I'd seen price tags as high as $2,000. I was surprised that even after several weeks, her owners hadn't shown up to take her home.

"I guess she's ours," I said to Colette one afternoon as she stood feeding the baby gray a slice of banana through her cage.

"No argument here," she said, pleased. "I'm all in favor of having a hospital mascot. But she needs a name."

We couldn't come up with anything more clever than the most obvious one, so we named her Target and moved her into a permanent Plexiglas cage in the waiting room with Stop, and the two female birds have been gossiping like girls and greeting visitors to the hospital ever since.

I FED BOTH birds and gave them a few strokes on their backs. Target began to whistle the theme to the *SpongeBob SquarePants*

TV show: "Who lives in a pineapple under the sea—Sponge-Bob SquarePants."

"Shhhh, it's much too early for that," I whispered as I stroked her.

Pet owners often ask why their birds talk so much. Parrot pets generally make a lot of noise because they are naturally very social animals. In the wild, they often live in flocks of hundreds. They forage for food, hunt for nest sites, and raise their offspring together, and through it all they talk, talk, talk. Many birds chatter all day, whether they are speaking unrecognizable "bird speak" or mimicking human language they've overheard or been taught. Klaus, an umbrella cockatoo—a large white parrot with a crest that opens like an umbrella—who often boards at the hospital, favors this greeting: "Hey, there, whatcha doin'?" in the deep voice of an older woman.

Since arriving at the hospital, Target had developed quite a repertoire of songs she picked up listening to the TV in the waiting room. She whistles the *SpongeBob* song the most, as well as a few others that all have the same tiresome quality of getting stuck in my head for exceedingly long stretches of time. Most recently, the theme song to *The Andy Griffith Show* has crept toward the top of her playlist. When Target's not singing, she and Stop have made a great game of parroting the chirping noises of every bird that comes through the front door, including cockatiels, lovebirds, and parakeets.

Once Target and Stop settled down, looking as though they might both fall back to sleep, I tiptoed away and into the main treatment room, where I'd moved both sugar gliders, Lily and Mathilda, for easy monitoring by the hospital staff and where the slightest change in their condition would be noticed. They were sleeping together, side by side, so that the stripes on one blended with the stripes on the other. I could scarcely tell where one began and the other ended. I ran a light finger along Mathilda's fur to see whether she'd absorbed the subcutaneous fluids we'd flowed through an injection drip into them overnight. All of the fluids were gone; yet her gums were still tacky and dry, and when I pulled the skin over her back, it stood up like a tent, indicating she was still dehydrated. They were both roused by my touch, so I pushed some pelleted food in front of them. Gliders tend to wake up ravenous, but neither seemed interested in eating, which indicated that their weakened state had not improved.

I left them to rest in the main treatment room and tried to tiptoe past the boarding room. Still, at the sound of my footsteps, the room came alive with high-pitched squawks and the scratch of scurrying feet. It wasn't quite breakfast time, but now that the overnight animals were awake, I knew I'd have to feed them or face a riot.

"Good morning, everyone," I said to a New Zealand white bunny and two long-haired Peruvian guinea pigs, a leopard gecko and a panther chameleon, and a peach-faced lovebird and a blue-and-gold macaw. "Who's hungry?" I lined up a series of bowls and filled them with veggies, insects, pellet food, and hay. Soon they were all happily munching—the birds making satisfied squawks, the guinea pigs hoarding and nibbling food in their hide boxes, the reptiles devouring insects whole. I closed the door to the boarding room and retreated to my office to begin making yet another round of difficult calls. Again Maxine was first on my list. I planned to ask her which mall she had adopted Georgie from. When she didn't answer, I left her a message.

"Maxine, I know this is a difficult time, but I may have learned something about Georgie's death that you could help me with. The information might explain what made him sick so that I can determine the cause of his death." I wavered, cognizant that what I said next might further upset her. "Maxine, I'm so sorry we lost Georgie, but you may be able to help me save other gliders who are sick. Please call me."

I went down my list of names, calling the other three owners of young gliders that had recently died under my care. No one picked up, so I left similar messages on one machine after the next. Then I waited.

8:45 A.M., MY OFFICE

MOST OF THE time an hour seems like an hour. Sometimes it seems like a lot more. This was one of those times. I could hear the hospital coming to life outside my office door. When I heard the familiar sound of the TV in the waiting room being turned on to Animal Planet, I knew Marnie had arrived. That cued Target and Stop to snap wide-awake and begin their battle over breakfast. Target would often push Stop off her favorite perch and hog the food. Stop would let out a deafening screech in protest. I took one final swig of my now cold cappuccino, pulled on my lab coat, and headed out to meet Marnie and Colette for rounds.

Marnie had already beat me to it and was standing outside examination room number three. "I was just about to head in," she said. "Thought I'd free you up this morning so you could keep an eye on Lily and Mathilda."

"Thanks," I said, "but their status is relatively unchanged, and I could use the distraction. Whom do we have in here?"

"Gillian and her four-year-old ferret, Jenson, are our first patients of the day." Marnie leaned forward and muttered, "I highly recommend a diet review."

I opened the door and greeted Gillian, who was dressed in electric pink yoga pants and a matching zip-up jacket. Dark hair framed her angled face, and her perfectly applied makeup was intact except for some smudged kohl black eyeliner under her eyes. I guessed she'd just come from the gym. She perched on the edge of the exam room chair, tapping her black Nike sneaker anxiously on the floor and holding a black-and-gray ferret that startled at my entry.

"This must be Jenson," I said to the lanky ferret, whose dark eyes were encircled by black fur like a mask. "Feel free to let him down on the floor."

Ferrets generally hate to be restrained. They're naturally playful, independent, and curious creatures that love to pounce, run, and hide.

"Oh, that's all right," she said without loosening her grip, "Jenson likes to be held."

He squirmed under her fingernails, and she clutched him tighter. It didn't seem to be a point worth arguing, so I just smiled and pulled up Jenson's chart on the computer screen.

"It says here you want to discuss Jenson's diet. What are your concerns?"

"Yes," she began quickly. "Jenson's always been a healthy eater, but lately he hardly even picks at anything. It's like he's not interested."

At the mention of food, my stomach growled, reminding me that I hadn't eaten since I'd left the house.

"My husband and I thought that maybe he was tired of his food, so I picked up a new brand. But then I worried that the new food might make him sick, so I switched him back to his old food." She shifted in her chair and began tapping her foot again; I got the feeling that many things worried Gillian.

"As long as you picked up one of the name brands specifically made for ferrets, I'm sure it's fine for him."

"Well, we weren't sure"—she waved a dismissive hand—"so we decided to wait."

"Wait, for—?"

"My husband thought we should try it first to see if it was okay."

I regarded her quizzically. "Do you mean you ate it . . . yourself?"

"Yes," she said, matter-of-factly. "We thought we should see how it settled with us before we gave it to him."

There are more than 8 million ferrets living in homes across the country, and I've treated my fair share of them, but this was the first time I'd met an owner who taste-tested her ferret's food. My eyes dropped down to the pockets on her warm-up jacket. I wondered if she had any on her now. Even as hungry as I was, I wasn't sure I could stomach ferret kibble.

"And?" I asked with genuine curiosity.

She shrugged. "Tastes like Kashi cereal."

I digested this information and then said, "Did it make you sick?"

"No, so we finally gave it to Jenson, but he's still not eating it."

"Okay, can I take a look at him?"

Gillian hesitated, holding fast to the thin, struggling animal. Was I going to have to pry him from her grip?

"I'll give him right back." I smiled and held out my hands.

She released her hold on Jenson and handed him over. His fur was smooth and long. I set the squirmy ferret on the examination table to palpate his belly before he wriggled through my hands. He slinked along the top of the exam table, his little pink nose and whiskers curiously sniffing and twitching.

"Jenson," she quietly scolded and began to reach for him.

"It's okay," I smiled. "He can't get very far in here."

Jenson dropped to the floor and squeezed his long body in between the wall and the exam table. Gillian watched him intently.

"He's a good weight and has great muscle tone," I said, "so I'm wondering if his poor appetite has to do with something else. What's the temperature in your home?"

Gillian finally looked up at me. "I keep the thermostat around eighty degrees in the winter. I hate being cold." She instinctively wrapped her arms around her slight frame. "Is that too low?"

"No, it's high."

I explained that while many small mammals feel comfortable at the same environmental temperatures as their owners, ferrets, along with rabbits, chinchillas, and guinea pigs, are a different story. They're sensitive to warm temperatures because their long and thick fur makes it difficult for them to release heat.

"Jenson's likely overheating, and this would explain why he's not eating."

Gillian looked at me quizzically.

"You know how it is when you're so hot in the summer, you don't want to eat?"

Gillian shrugged. "I try not to eat a lot anyway."

"Well, either way, I recommend turning down the heat. No higher than seventy-five degrees, and if there's a room in your house that tends to be cooler than the rest, move Jensen's cage in there so he can, you know, chill."

Gillian ignored my attempt to sound cool. "And what do I do about the food?" she asked eagerly.

"Stop eating it."

I stepped out into the hall, savoring the image of Gillian eating handfuls of high-protein ferret food before heading to a ninety-minute spin class to burn off the calories. My stomach rumbled again, and I felt light-headed. I knew better than to ignore the signs; I had to quickly grab a snack.

THEY SAY THAT caregivers—nurses, doctors, and most people in a medical profession—often overlook self-care. We look after our patients and forget about ourselves. This is certainly true of me. I push myself as hard as I can for the animals in my care and don't make much time for my own rest and rejuvenation. I used to think this constant tendency to be in overdrive was just a by-product of living in Manhattan until I recognized that many of my city friends took time to slow down, at least on the weekends. I finally had to admit that my frantic pace was more about me than where I lived. Still, Peter and I hoped that by leaving the hustle and bustle of New York City for the quieter, calmer countryside of Westchester County, we would naturally unwind and create that idyllic home we wanted for our future family. The move did slow me down, but I didn't make my health a daily priority right away.

For the first few years we lived in Mount Kisco, Peter commuted in and out of Manhattan on the Metro-North train, leaving early in the morning and often not getting home until long after the sun had set. I was working nearly full-time, too, rotating on-call shifts at various veterinary hospitals in the area, while also caring for a two-year-old toddler and a newborn baby.

One evening, after picking up young Brett and baby Luke from a sitter's down the street, I pulled up to our dark house. Scolding myself for having forgotten to turn on the porch lights, I unloaded the car and the boys in the darkness and fumbled to find the keyhole to open the door without loosening my hold on Luke. Once we finally got inside, I flipped on switch after switch, but we were still standing in darkness. Had we suffered a power outage? Had a fuse blown? After stumbling around in the dark with an infant on my hip and a whiney toddler trailing behind, I wondered if perhaps I'd forgotten to pay the electric bill. It sounded like the beginning of a great joke. What happens when a doctor and a lawyer don't pay their electric bill? The same thing that happens to everyone who doesn't pay: the lights go out.

I let out a series of G-rated expletives and then went searching for candles. If you could see the unspoken words between almost any husband and wife hanging in the air like in bubbles in a comic strip, they would read like this: "Why don't you do something about this?" followed by "Why don't *you* do something about this?" Feeling my way through the darkness, I found myself getting more and more resentful that Peter was not home to solve our problem. But by the next night, the lights were back on, and Peter and I were sharing an exhausted laugh over it as we lay collapsed together in a heap on the couch. The boys, the birds, and the cats were asleep. The house was quiet, and it was just us.

"I can just picture you"—Peter grinned—"trying to remain calm for Brett and Luke while cursing under your breath when you couldn't find the emergency flashlight."

"I never did find it. Thank goodness for Brett's toy police car. We used the flashing siren to make our way upstairs."

"I though you hated that toy."

I did hate that toy. I had scolded my mom for giving it to Brett for his birthday. The siren was loud enough to wake the dead.

"Well, who knew it would actually come in handy?" I relented.

Peter took two sandwiches out of a paper bag and handed one to me. "Dinner?"

"At least it's together," I said with a smile. "Even if it's just sandwiches."

"Just sandwiches?" Peter took mock offense, unwrapping his pastrami. "Only from the best deli in Mount Kisco." He took a bite. "Mmmm, these are almost as good as the sandwiches we used to get from the deli on Avenue B."

"That good, huh?" I unwrapped my turkey club. Peter's enthusiasm for the simple things in life is infectious. Deli sandwiches shared together on our living room couch suddenly felt as decadent as dining in Paris along the Seine. I leaned back against him. We were both so tired. Peter had dark hollows under his eyes, and I didn't look much better. We gobbled our sandwiches in silence.

"I was thinking," he finally said. "What if I made sure that the next time this happens, I'm here with you?"

I thought back to the night before, when I had wanted nothing more than for Peter to walk through the door and help me. I said, "There's not going to be another time. I have all the bills set to autopay now. Even if I forget to pay them, the computer won't."

"Online banking. Wow, you're really at the forefront of technology," he teased. I turned and gave him a light punch on the shoulder.

"I mean it, though," Peter said more seriously. "Situations like this are bound to keep coming up where you need me closer to home. What if I cut back my hours at the office?"

I tensed, and Peter could feel it.

"Let me guess," he sighed. "You don't like the idea."

I took in a deep breath, but before I could respond Peter continued, "I know it wasn't 'the plan,' but I want you to think about what we're doing. We're both killing ourselves nearly every day. I'm exhausted. You're exhausted. It's not good for our family, and"—he paused—"I worry about your health."

Peter had a legitimate concern. Between work and running after two little boys, my health often slipped down the day's priority list. I'd become less disciplined about exercising regularly and eating balanced meals, and unless I was making dinner for the family, I sometimes skipped eating altogether. If I were to be honest, it would be helpful to have Peter home more. But I feared it would come at a cost to my career.

I reminded Peter, "We agreed that you'd continue to work full-time at the firm while I worked to build up a loyal clientele of exotic pet owners in the area. I can't open my own hospital without a solid list."

"Yes, I know that was our agreement," Peter said steadily, "but what if we both cut back, just a little bit?"

I crossed my arms and slowly shook my head. "No, I'm not willing to do that. I'm so close. I've worked so hard."

Peter and I sat in silence for several minutes. Finally he said, "Laurie, I've always supported you, and I will never ask you to give up your dream. I'm simply suggesting that you put it on hold. I know you don't want to hear this, but, honey, you just can't do it all."

No matter how right Peter was, I wasn't ready to admit it.

I turned toward him and appealed, "Don't cut back your hours yet. Give me a few more months to drum up clients. I can do it. Just a few more months at this pace, and then, I promise, we can both relax."

Peter took a deep breath. He sat for a moment and then reluctantly agreed. The next morning, he caught the early train, as usual, into Manhattan; I dropped Brett at preschool and Luke at the sitter's and left for the animal hospital in Rockland County where I worked one day a week. We didn't resume our conversation again until nearly six months later when a nurse called him from the local hospital to tell him I'd passed out.

I was lying on an examination table, my eyelids as heavy as rocks, when I finally pushed them open. Peter was standing next to me with a bouquet of lavender tulips and a large Starbucks coffee. "This oughta wake you up," he said, smiling. He was trying to be funny, but his eyes were worried and pinched. I knew he was scared. He sat down on the edge of the table.

"I spoke with your doctor." His voice was serious now. "You collapsed from hypoglycemia and . . . " Peter paused as if he were holding something back.

"What?" I whimpered.

"Laurie"—he took my hand—"you've been diagnosed with adult-onset type 1 diabetes." Peter squeezed my hand. "If you won't listen to me, please, listen to your doctor. Listen to your *body*."

I looked down at my thin outline tucked under a blanket, an IV stuck in my skinny arm. How long had I been out? How did I get here? Where were the boys?

Tears welled up in my eyes. Peter was right. *I give.*

"Okay," I said quietly, "you're right. I'll stop. I can't do it all."

"You can do *a lot.*" Peter squeezed my hand. "Just not everything all at once."

"I'll take some time off," I promised as tears ran down my cheeks. "But don't get used to it," I whimpered and then narrowed my eyes at him. "I'm not giving up on my career."

"No." Peter smiled and kissed me on the lips. "No doubt about that, Doctor. Plus, it won't take long before the boys and I get tired of having you home so much."

10:18 A.M., MAIN TREATMENT ROOM

As I NIBBLED on my protein bar, I revisited the memory of that pivotal moment in my health, my career, and my marriage. So many of us get married and start new lives, not realizing that there will likely be hidden costs we hadn't envisioned—compromises we'll have to make, dreams, pastimes, habits we'll be asked to leave behind in order to forge a new path ahead with our spouse or partner. When I conceded that I would have to put my career on hold in order to take care of my health and my family, I feared I was giving up my professional dream, choosing one love over another. But looking back now, I realized that wasn't true. I had just postponed the opening of the animal hospital for a few years. The timing of my plans shifted, but Peter had never actually asked me to give anything up. And I hadn't.

Bob Dixon, I now understood, had similarly tried to make compromises to maintain the peace in his marriage over the years. But now his treasured sugar gliders were sick and quite possibly dying, and it appeared that he still felt he had to keep their treatment a secret from his wife. *Or what?* I wondered. Would she deny treatment, as Susan Mitchell had feared her husband would do when he learned about her guinea pig Rosie's dire condition?

I looked down into Lily and Mathilda's cage. The younger glider had reduced herself to a small lump, and her lids were drawn tautly over her eyes. Lily was protectively snuggled up next to her.

Marnie walked up behind me. I shook my head and said, "It's happening all over again. Her system is beginning to shut down."

If Mathilda was on the same trajectory and timetable as Georgie, she would die in a matter of days.

"I have to call Bob."

I stepped outside the main treatment room and dialed his number from my private cell phone. He answered on the first ring.

"It's Dr. Hess," I said, "and I know you don't want me to call you directly, but it couldn't wait. It's Mathilda. I need you to come in right away."

As I waited for Bob to drive the thirty minutes it would take him to arrive at the hospital, I determined that I had time to meet with one more patient. A very special patient: Bennie Weston and his chinchillas. Bennie would be a welcome reprieve on a day when grim news was becoming the theme.

I swung open the door of examination room number two. "Hi, Bennie!"

A heavyset, middle-aged man looked down at the ground and softly muttered a hello. His elderly mother, Sheila, and I exchanged a delighted smile. After all, less than a year ago, Bennie's mother had still been doing all the talking for him.

"How are the guys?" I knelt down in front of a cage housing three fuzzy gray-and-black chinchillas. Bennie had adopted the trio from a nearby shelter when they were babies.

"Their names are Gigabyte, Megabyte, and Mac," Bennie said matter-of-factly. "Don't you remember?"

"Yes, of course, I remember," I said with a smile. "How could I forget?"

Bennie had Asperger's syndrome, and although he was highly functioning when it came to caring for his pets, socially he could be as nervous and withdrawn as a chinchilla. Sheila once explained out of earshot of her son, "It's like Bennie was born into a world where everyone has the owner's manual but him. He tries very hard to fit in, but it's difficult. Those animals love him though," she said tenderly. "For whatever reason, he's able to connect with those funny little fur balls in a way that he can't do with the rest of us."

I understood that Gigabyte, Megabyte, and Mac were able to reach that place inside Bennie that was closed and inaccessible to all others, including his mother. I watched as Bennie spoke in a soft and intimate way to his three animals in their cage. I'd seen this sort of special connection to animals before among other children and adults with developmental issues. I'd witnessed in the hospital what many studies have also shown—that people on the autistic spectrum can relax, communicate, and interact with their pets, when they can't easily do the same with people.

Even with his Asperger's, I thought, Bennie really wasn't that different from anyone else. We all crave that special friend whom we can connect with, whether it's a chinchilla, a sugar glider, or a pionus parrot. Bennie had found his, and today Bennie's three companions were huddled so shyly in the corner of their carrier that I could hardly pry them out.

"Let me," Bennie said. As he pulled them out, one by one, their bodies relaxed as they recognized Bennie's hands and gentle voice.

"It's okay, friends," he assured them. "Doctor Hess just wants to examine you." He slowly handed me his chinchillas, one at a time, and I held each close to my body as I examined them, head to tail, paying careful attention to their teeth. I always make it a priority to thoroughly examine a chinchilla's mouth. These small rodents are known for developing dental problems because their teeth continue to grow throughout their lifetimes, and the incisors' roots are particularly long. Chinchillas consume rough grasses and shrubs in the wild, which helps wear down their teeth naturally so that they stay healthy. But captive chinchillas are often fed only pellets, so their teeth can become overgrown and easily become impacted.

"I think Mac is eating more than the others," Bennie said. Then he paused as if he were carefully formulating his next thought. "I weighed him this morning, and he's over the appropriate level."

Bennie made a habit of weighing his chinchillas every morning and carefully measured their food. This wasn't necessary—the rodents weren't on the Weight Watchers plan—but the daily ritual made Bennie feel more in control of his environment.

"I bet he's just fine, Bennie, but let's weigh him on my scale just to be sure." Sheila nodded at her son, legitimizing his concerns, and Bennie walked over and placed Mac on the scale, intently watching the reading.

"See there. One and a half pounds," I said. "Mac seems to be at the correct weight, but remember when we discussed digestion and how weight fluctuates during the day? Depending on what time Mac eats, his weight will change a little."

Bennie nodded that he understood.

"Everything looks just as it should. You're doing a fantastic job," I said.

"I'm doing a fantastic job," Bennie repeated quietly under his breath.

Marnie poked her head into the examination room. "Hi, Bennie. Hi, Mrs. Weston. Sorry to interrupt, but when you're finished, Laurie, Bob is here."

Bennie perked up. "Can I go see Colette now?"

Sheila and I exchanged delighted looks.

"Bennie makes his own appointments now," Sheila said proudly.

Mrs. Weston slowly lifted herself up out of her chair. I noticed her putting her hands on her knees and hesitating for a moment before she pushed herself up to a standing position. She reached for the cage, but Bennie stepped in front of her.

"No, Mom. I will get it." He picked up the cage and then opened the examination door for his mother.

"Thank you, son." She patted his arm and slowly stepped forward.

Not so long ago, Bennie wouldn't have noticed that his mother needed help, not because he didn't care for her but because other people's needs weren't on his radar. I had no doubt that Bennie's expression of empathy now was the direct result of learning to tend to Gigabyte, Megabyte, and Mac.

I joined Marnie in the main treatment room, where Bob was hunched over Lily and Mathilda's cage. He straightened up when he heard me enter.

"Thank you for getting here so fast," I said. "I didn't think it could wait."

"I've explained Mathilda's progressive paralysis and weakness to Bob," Marnie said, "but I think he has a few more questions."

"I don't understand," Bob said helplessly. "Why is this happening to her?"

My heart ached. Maxine had asked me the same thing.

"There's something you should know," I said gently.

Bob looked anxiously from me to Marnie. "What is it?"

"Mathilda is exhibiting equivalent symptoms to four other sugar gliders I've recently treated at the hospital." I paused and looked at Marnie, who gave me an encouraging nod. "I regret to say that so far, not one of them has survived."

The color drained out of Bob's face.

1:00 P.M., MY OFFICE

THE DAY WAS hardly halfway over, and I just wanted to pack up, go home to my family, and take some downtime to think. I'd spent over an hour with Bob, recounting everything I knew and was still investigating about the unexplained sugar glider deaths. As expected, he was alarmed by how quickly the sickness was spreading, and he was frightened for Lily and Mathilda. I'd assured him I was doing everything in my power to determine the cause of the sickness before it took another life. Whereas someone else might have condemned me for my inadequacy and what was beginning to feel like failure, Bob had simply said, "I trust you. Do whatever you can." This is perhaps the biggest compliment a veterinarian can get from a pet owner, and Bob's faith in me created an even greater sense of urgency. *What else could I do to help this man and his gliders?*

As I slumped down in my office chair and nervously ran a hand through my hair, I noticed the message light blinking on my office phone. I felt a surge of both anticipation and apprehension. I reached out and pressed play.

"Hello, Dr. Hess." I recognized the voice immediately. It was Mr. Huntington. "My granddaughter's sugar glider, Pockets, recently passed away at your hospital. You said in your voice mail that you wanted to know where Pockets came from."

I leaned forward and held my breath.

"I bought him at the Johnson Valley Mall."

3

A CONNECTION

First thing the next morning, I dumped a cup of cat food into the cat feeder in my kitchen. Gizmo, Tilly, Bean, and Bingo threaded themselves through my legs.

"How did I end up with so many cats?" I muttered aloud to myself.

Of course, I knew the answer. They'd entered the house in stages. We'd adopted Bean, the friendliest and also the most senseless cat, from the SPCA. He'd chased his own shadow for nearly a year until I went looking to find him a buddy. I found two—Bingo and Gizmo, both huge and feral. I'd seen a listing in the local *Penny Saver* from a woman in upstate New York. I answered the ad, and she invited me to her house where I met over a dozen strays living in her small laundry room. I singled out Bingo, who seemed the most docile, but his hissing and spitting brother Gizmo wouldn't let me near him.

"Looks like you'll have to take them both," said the owner of the animals. "Keep the siblings together, right?"

It was a logical and caring consideration, but I'd only really wanted one cat, and now she was asking me to take on a second—Bingo's surly sidekick.

I finally acquiesced. But to get both cats to leave their well-insulated den behind the washing machine, I had to fish them out, hissing and scratching, with a net. I wrestled them both into a cardboard box that I literally had to tape shut. As I drove home with both cats mewling loudly in the back seat, I wondered what had I gotten myself into.

The two siblings lived in a small crate in my bathroom for a month and then in isolation in my bedroom for nearly another twelve. With time and much patience, Gizmo and Bingo eventually became socialized creatures and joined the rest of the household. Ironically, Gizmo softened the most— he often follows me from room to room like a loyal dog. Tilly, our Maine coon and only female pet, joined the pack only after Bean, Gizmo, and Bingo had learned to get along harmoniously. Maine coons are one of the largest breeds of house cat. They have big feet and long, luxurious fur. They're known to have sweet temperaments, and with people, Tilly certainly does. She loves to be around us and roams from room to room meowing until she finds someone to adore her. But when it comes to her male counterparts, she treats them like mere annoyances. She politely interacts during mealtime and then retreats to the guest bedroom, the quietest room in the house. Unless someone is visiting from out of town, Tilly claims the room as her own. I often find her there, sprawled on the queen-size bed or nestled underneath a heap of antique quilts.

I stepped around my pride of felines without tripping, a move that's taken me years of practice, as Peter walked into the kitchen. I handed him a cup of coffee.

"Did I tell you that my old intern Elliot showed up again at my office yesterday afternoon? Poor guy, I think I scared him to death," I said as Peter sat down at the kitchen table.

"You can be pretty scary," Peter teased. "Can't she, Dale?" Dale looked up from his regular morning perch on Peter's right shoulder and chirped in agreement.

"Don't bring Dale into this."

Peter looked at Dale and shrugged. "Someone hasn't had her coffee yet." Dale chirped again, and Peter gave him a handful of pelleted bird food and seeds and then tossed some out toward the cats. Bingo pounced on a sunflower seed just as Tilly lumbered over and pushed him out of the way.

It's easy to forget that Dale is my bird, the way those two act together—they're practically inseparable. Who would believe that before we met Peter had an aversion to birds? I threw a dish towel in their direction, and they both squawked. This was our typical morning exchange. Once Brett and Luke catch the bus to Twin Pines Middle School, and before I run to the gym and Peter heads to the train, we try to give ourselves a few moments of playful time together.

"So what'd he want?" Peter asked as he unfolded the *New York Times*.

I thought back to my encounter with Elliot the day before. I'd been playing Mr. Huntington's message confirming that Pockets had come from Johnson Valley Mall.

A deep voice behind me said, "Dr. Hess?" and I spun around in my chair. "What are you doing here?" I'd nearly shrieked when I saw Elliot standing in the doorway.

"Sorry," he stammered and took a step backward. "I'll come back later," he said and disappeared into the hall.

"Elliot, no, wait a minute," I called after him once my heart stopped racing. "You surprised me, that's all. Come back. I'm sorry."

He hesitantly reappeared, and I waved him forward. "Come in, please."

At the kitchen table, I said to Peter, "He asked if he could help me around the hospital until after the holidays, when he will return to his internship in Rhode Island." I took a sip of my coffee. "So I gave him a job."

"That's great. You've been wanting someone to help you organize the hospital inventory and scan medical records, right?"

"Well, yes, I do need help in the back office, but I'm going to use Elliot for something else." Peter looked up with interest.

"For what?"

"Elliot's going to help me chase down leads on Sugar Buddies."

Peter frowned. "I thought I was your lead investigator?"

"Honey"—I smiled and reached for his hand—"you are definitely my top guy, but need I remind you that you already have a full-time job? Elliot's in town for holiday break with nothing to do except entertain his pet snake."

"Elliot has a snake now?"

"That's another story." I finished my coffee and stood up from the table. "I'll fill you in later. Elliot's meeting me at the hospital in ten minutes, and then we're heading out to Johnson Valley Mall."

"Who's covering your morning rounds?"

"Marnie. A gecko, three rabbits, and a chicken in for hormone therapy." I leaned in and gave him a kiss on the cheek.

"Between the two of you, I don't know who takes better care of me." I headed for the back door.

"I do," he called out.

As I walked toward the Highlander, careful not to slip on the slick driveway, I considered that although Peter has my back, it's really Marnie who holds my hand. Not only is she my right-hand tech who can anticipate my every move, but she's also one of my closest friends. For over ten years now, we've seen each other through it all: challenging career moves, marriage proposals, pregnancies, illness, and divorce.

We first met at the Bedford Specialty Center after I moved upstate. We recognized in each other a wild passion for animal medicine. Also, we both had young children so we had even more in common. As I moved around the county, clocking in hours at a number of animal hospitals and building a clientele to one day support my own, Marnie followed right along with me. The day we opened the doors of the Veterinary Center for Birds & Exotics, she stood right beside me, scissors in hand. Together we cut the red ribbon and proudly welcomed pets and their owners into our care.

We performed our first major surgery together on Daisy, a five-foot-long and very pregnant iguana. Daisy had arrived at the hospital with a belly full of infertile eggs that she couldn't lay, a condition called egg binding in which one or more eggs get stuck along the way, which can kill the animal.

Daisy's well-intentioned owner, seventy-two-year-old Bernice, had severe emphysema and required an oxygen tank to get from one room to another. Bernice was frail, but when her pet became too sick to move, she somehow managed to lift the pregnant lizard into her Buick and drive three hours upstate to my hospital, wearing her oxygen mask the entire way.

I was pretty certain that in Daisy's case, the egg binding resulted from vitamin D and calcium deficiencies. Iguanas in captivity rarely get the direct sun exposure they require to make vitamin D. If they can't be outside, they usually need several hours a day under artificial ultraviolet lights to get the amount they need. Daisy appeared to be deficient in the essential vitamins, which meant she couldn't absorb enough calcium from her food to help her muscles contract and pass out the eggs. I started her on calcium and lubricants to get her eggs to pass, but it quickly became apparent that her condition was dire, and we had to prep the iguana for surgery. Bernice went home to wait.

The moment I incised Daisy's abdomen, Marnie and I could see a web of tiny blood vessels feeding her oviducts and the three dozen eggs they contained. This would be no simple surgery. As we clamped off one minuscule blood vessel at a time, the vessels began to bleed. No matter how we tied them off—whether it was with sutures or special surgical staples called Hemoclips, Daisy continued to hemorrhage. I couldn't understand why Daisy was bleeding so heavily. After four hours in surgery, we'd removed all the eggs, but Daisy had lost a tremendous amount of blood, and her gums were pale, indicating that she'd become dangerously anemic. Marnie was trying desperately to keep Daisy's blood pressure up with intravenous fluids and blood plasma substitutes, but Daisy eventually stopped breathing on her own. She was limp as a dishrag as we inserted a breathing tube down her trachea. We had to jostle her every few minutes to stimulate breathing. After an hour of this, I looked at Marnie; she looked at me; sweat dripped from both of our foreheads. To survive, Daisy needed a blood donor, and it's not as though donor iguanas are out cruising the hallways of the animal hospital. I scrubbed out of surgery, leaving Marnie to continue stimulating Daisy's breathing, to phone Bernice and tell her that I was doing all I could, but it was likely Daisy would die.

"Oh, please don't give up on her, Dr. Hess," she wheezed. "She's all I have."

Exhausted and weary, I trudged back to the operating room and told Marnie we weren't giving up. We replaced the tube in Daisy's airway and continued to administer oxygen, along with Oxyglobin, a blood substitute. We canceled all of our afternoon appointments so that we could focus our energy and attention on saving Daisy. At that point, however, we couldn't do much more than wait. One hour. Two hours. Still no movement or breathing on her own. Marnie supported me through those long hours, encouraging us both to persevere. We were nearly ready to give up and go home, when suddenly Daisy took a breath. One breath, then another. Shallow at first, then much deeper and stronger. Bernice's old, muscle-wasted lizard, who had been all but dead, was slowly coming back to life. Marnie and I stared at Daisy in disbelief and then burst into sloppy, tearful laughter and hugged each other tight.

8:05 A.M., ANIMAL HOSPITAL

I WAS PULLING into the hospital parking lot when my phone buzzed. It was a text from Peter: "Don't forget Brett's soccer practice—4pm."

I hadn't needed the reminder. The event was in my calendar, and I planned to be there, although I really didn't want to be. I felt awful admitting this to myself, but attending my sons' practices was like torture for me. While I love watching

Brett and Luke play sports (they're both natural athletes), the rivalry on the sidelines often leaves me feeling as if I've been kicked in the shins. I still hadn't recovered from the last game I'd attended earlier in the season. I'd shown up with Vitamin-waters and energy bars for the boys. My neighbor Katherine, who was still pregnant then, had somehow stretched her son Gilman's team T-shirt over her swollen belly. I willed a smile when I saw her on the edge of the field and waved. We weren't friends, but we were neighbors. I reminded myself of what Peter always says: *be nice.* Katherine waddled hastily toward me.

"I'm surprised to see you here," she said in a chiding tone. "I was sure you'd be working again today."

"I was," I said lightly, "and now I'm here."

She cast a disapproving look at my plastic bag from Duane Reade. "You know, a cooler holds a lot more drinks. That way, every child on the team can have one."

"Oh, I didn't know I was supposed to—"

"You were probably in a hurry to get here from work," she waved me off. "Maybe next time you can bring something for everyone. The team plays better when everyone is hydrated."

I felt the hairs on the back of my neck stand up as Katherine brushed past me to join a group of parents grilling hot dogs and hamburgers at the far end of the benches. I stood abandoned on the sidelines with my pathetic bag of drinks. I was just about to retreat to a solitary bench on the other end of the field when I heard the players erupt, "Awesome, Mozo!" Brett—fondly called "Mozo" by his teammates because it's short for his last name, Mozarsky—had just scored a goal.

"Nice play!" I yelled, clapping wildly.

Brett tends to be hyperfocused and stoic on the field, but when he heard my voice, he looked over and gave a smile.

That little exchange made Katherine's cutting words fade away—until later that night when I grumbled to Peter, "So sue me. I didn't know I was responsible for hydrating the *entire team*. She acted like I was some monster denying our kids their basic human rights."

"Water is essential to survival," Peter cracked.

"Ugh, I will never win with that woman," I said, bristling.

"Maybe not," Peter shrugged. Then he brightened. "But we know who does win—MOZO!"

I returned his smile. Peter always knows how to cheer me up.

Since then, Peter had offered to attend most practices and games even though it meant taking an early train home. Katherine couldn't have been happier. Peter, much more gregarious than I am, is an easy crowd pleaser.

But today Peter had a late-afternoon call scheduled with his West Coast office. The time difference would keep him late in the city, so Katherine and her neighborhood coterie would have to settle for me.

"And don't forget the drinks," Peter texted, with an emoticon wink.

10:00 A.M., TACONIC STATE PARKWAY

AS ELLIOT AND I rode out to Johnson Valley Mall, we relived some of our more memorable cases together.

"Remember Ninna and her wild toad from Barbados?" Elliot asked.

"You mean her illegal and poisonous toad?" I said. "I remember feeling so protective of the interns and the staff, but you were practically sparring with each other to get into the examination room with me."

"Can you blame us? As far as exotic animals go, there's not much more exotic than that."

While traveling in her native Barbados, Ninna had illegally captured two bufo toads in the woods surrounding her hotel. She hid the small amphibians in an instant coffee can that she stuffed under clothing and souvenirs in her suitcase and flew them back with her to New York City. Unlike Ninna, who had adapted to a new country, the toads were suddenly strangers in a strange land, and Ninna had no idea what they needed in order to survive. In less than a week, one of the toads had died, and when the other began to exhibit signs of illness, Ninna took the toad on the train from Manhattan to our hospital in Westchester, where she hoped I would help.

As soon as Ninna peeled back the lid of her coffee can, I recognized the wrinkly animal as a bufo toad, also known as a giant toad because it can grow to over two pounds and as long as four to six inches.

"Do you know what you have here?" I asked her.

"I know it's big and ugly," she said, "but kind of cute, too. No?"

"This is a bufo toad, and it's very sick." I could tell by its large, sunken eyes and droopy eyelids that it was weak. It was also motionless and bloated, which indicated that it was dehydrated.

"Also," I said, "it's extremely poisonous."

"It *is*?"

"See this," I said pointing to the wart-like glands that protruded from the skin behind its eyes. "When threatened, a bufo will secrete a white, fatty, and very poisonous toxin from these glands to deter its predator."

I asked Marnie to run and grab me a special pair of moist-
ened rubber gloves, a paper gown, and protective goggles. I
was soon outfitted like a character from the movie *Outbreak*.

I explained to Ninna, "Their skin toxin is highly dangerous
to other animals, and it can be equally irritating to human
skin. I'm surprised you haven't already suffered burns from
handling him."

She held up her hands. They were indeed pink and swollen.

"I thought it was from the chilies in my Bajan Pepper Pot.
My recipe is extra spicy."

I wanted to scold Ninna for adding one more bufo toad
to a growing problem. Tropical bufo toads like Ninna's had
become an invasive species, specifically in Florida, where they
were outcompeting the native species, and also there were reports that their toxic venom was killing dogs, cats, and other
animals that came in contact with them. For this reason, I
do not recommend bufo toads as pets. A fire-bellied toad or
a White's tree frog is so much friendlier—and cuter, in my
opinion. But what could I do? Ninna had illegally poached
the animal from its native habitat, and now here it was on
my examination table. I could deny treatment of the animal,
but then she'd likely release it back into the wild where it
probably wouldn't survive, or if it went untreated in her care,
it would likely die in the bottom of the coffee can—neither
of which, as far as I was concerned, was an acceptable option.

I try not to get too preachy on this point, but as a veterinary doctor, I feel it is my responsibility to provide animals—
whatever they are—with the care they need to thrive in
captivity. Of course there are some exceptions to this rule,
such as treating extremely venomous animals like a sick rat-
tlesnake, which has a deadly bite and needs to be properly

restrained to protect me and my staff. I simply don't have the equipment necessary to treat a poisonous snake like that.

Ninna's bufo fell into a gray area. The toad was poisonous but not venomous, and I did have the proper tools to treat him safely. I took another look at the parched and withered toad, knowing full well that amphibians can go downhill quickly once they stop eating and lose a significant amount of water weight. I decided to treat him.

"The first thing I will do is run some diagnostic tests," I said to Ninna. Amphibians can be difficult to perform tests on, as they don't have readily accessible veins, so I carefully drained a small amount of fluid from under the bufo's skin to culture it and have it examined microscopically at the lab. Then I administered an injection of antibiotics and an oral calcium supplement pending the test results.

"Take your toad home, and I will call you as soon as I have test results," I instructed Ninna. "He'll need a temperature-controlled and humidity-controlled tank with ultraviolet light and heat. He will not survive in this coffee can." I handed her a pair of gloves. "And remember, handle this animal with extreme care."

I TOOK THE Maple Avenue exit off the freeway and pulled into the Johnson Valley Mall parking lot. It was already jammed.

"Holiday shopping," I groaned. "Prepare to be pushed around in the name of good cheer."

Elliot and I trudged through the crowded Sears, passing flat-screen televisions trimmed in silver garland and Craftsman tools wrapped in bright holiday bows. We emerged into the mall's central corridor, which smelled like my grandmother's cupboard throuhout Hanukkah: vanilla, cinnamon, and brown sugar. I glanced at Elliot, who was humming along to Kelly Clarkson's rocky rendition of "Run Run Rudolph."

"Mr. Huntington said he bought Pockets at a kiosk just outside Sears," I said, looking to my left and right. There were vendors selling sunglasses, cell phone sleeves, e-cigarettes, and remote-controlled monster trucks.

"I don't see any sugar gliders," Elliot said. "Should we ask?" He pointed toward the information desk.

Elliot and I approached a twenty-something woman with candy cane lips and blond curls tucked under a Santa hat. She smiled and crinkled her nose—nonverbal confirmation that she was a helpful elf.

"I'm looking for a vendor called Sugar Buddies." I said. "Do you know where it is?"

"Sugar what?" She twirled a chunky piece of hair around her finger.

"They sell mar-su-pee-als," I enunciated. As the last consonant slipped out of my mouth, her cheery disposition faded. I could see that I'd insulted her by sounding like a snooty schoolteacher, and before I could apologize, she said, "Ma'am, I can spell, but I don't know that word you're looking for."

Elliot took a jaunty step forward and pointed at her name tag. "Hi—Jackie, is it?"

She happily shifted her attention from me and nodded at Elliot.

"We're looking for a pet vendor," he explained. "They sell animals called sugar gliders."

"Oh," she said, lighting up again, now with recognition. "Are those the flying squirrels?"

"It's a gliding membrane that allows them to fly," I interjected.

Jackie glanced back at me with a look like, *Why are you still talking?*

Oops, I couldn't help myself. I was just so anxious for answers. I closed my mouth and stepped back, grateful that I'd brought Elliot along. With his friendly face and easy temperament, he never offends anyone.

"What she means," Elliot said with a grin, "is that they do look like flying squirrels."

"That's what I thought. It's a squirrel with a monkey tail, right?" She rolled her eyes at me. "It's like, I know what I saw."

"So you've seen them?" Elliot asked.

Jackie leaned forward and lowered her voice. "The mall had to add extra security just to keep the crowds under control. They were jumping and flying all over the place. The kids were going nuts over those squirrels." She stopped and giggled. "Nuts over squirrels, that's funny."

"They are very popular," Elliot agreed. "'Most Popular Exotic Pet,' says *People* magazine."

"Really?" Jackie was wide-eyed.

Elliot was flirting. He doesn't even read *People*. I cleared my throat, and Elliot picked up on my cue.

"So, hey, Jackie, do you know where we can find the flying squirrels?"

"Oh, they're gone now," she said with a pout. "Packed up two days ago."

Elliot mirrored her disappointment and asked, "Any idea where they went?"

"Not a clue."

I could feel my body deflate, and I let out a sigh. Without seeing the kiosk, I couldn't determine if anything about the gliders' care or display might be causing the illness that was making them sick. Now what? I could continue to play private investigator, but that would take more time—minutes, hours, and potentially more days that I was running out of. Mathilda's health was declining; she was on borrowed time.

Jackie tilted her head, and the silver bell on the tip of her hat made a jingling sound. "I did overhear someone say that the flying squirrels came from some farm outside town." She giggled again. "Like they're cows or something." Elliot and I exchanged a knowing glance.

"Thank you," I said. I could understand why Jackie found the comparison between a cow and a sugar glider laughable, but exotic animals are often raised on farms in large numbers, just like cows.

In fact, breeding farms like what Jackie had described exist all across the world, depending on the species. I was already familiar with a facility in upstate New York that breeds and supplies the majority of ferrets to pet stores across the country. I'd also heard about a smaller farm in Putnam County that breeds mini pigs. Often these farms are in undisclosed places that companies don't advertise so as not to draw public attention to them. Farms that breed animals for sale are often referred to as "mills" and receive unfavorable attention and criticism, given that so many pets are abandoned at shelters and in need of rescue and new homes. I try not to take a political position either way and instead focus on what I'm trained to do: provide treatment and save lives.

As soon as we were back in the car, I asked Elliot, "Do an online search for 'Sugar Buddies.' See if their company website states where they breed their gliders."

"Sure thing, Dr. Hess." A few taps later, Elliot announced, "There's an address here for a corporate office in Fairfield County."

"That's in Connecticut. Less than an hour away."

"You think that's actually the farm where they breed the animals?"

"We'll find out."

I was beginning to feel hopeful again. I quickly called Marnie to check in on Lily and Mathilda.

"How are the girls?"

"Weak but holding steady."

"And how are you?"

"Oh, you know, just another exciting day at the animal hospital. Harlow the hedgehog is in the waiting room, itching himself all over. And I mean, *all over*. He's managed to contort himself into positions I didn't think were even possible. It's the hedgehog version of Cirque du Soleil. Impressive, really."

I tried to picture it. Hedgehogs aren't the most flexible or agile creatures. They have short, skimpy legs, and like porcupines, they're covered in sharp quills all over their back to deter predators from picking them up. When they roll themselves defensively into a tight ball—their signature move—they look like Weebles, the wobbling kids' toys popular in the 1970s. Captive hedgehogs are especially unsteady, as they tend to be housed in cages with little opportunity to exercise and they love to overeat. I've been putting portly hedgehogs on crash diets ever since I started my practice.

"What's he in for?"

"Irritable itching."

"Really, is that a new medical term?"

"That's what Gerry and Kurt are calling it." I could hear her amusement over the phone.

"Well, I'm sure it's nothing serious. Probably just mites. A simple shot will take care of that."

"Ha! Try telling Gerry that."

Gerry had gotten so anxious waiting for Harlow's test results the last time he visited the hospital that I thought he might hyperventilate.

"I promise we'll be back soon. In the meantime, try to keep Gerry calm."

"I have a paper bag ready."

I'd previously treated Harlow for "excess saliva," another medical term Kurt and Gerry had made up. They came bursting through the hospital doors one afternoon and insisted I draw blood and "test for everything." Gerry held out a foaming Harlow and extended him toward me. Handling a nervous hedgehog can be tricky, as the animal will tend to twitch and contract the muscles on its back, raising its usually flattened quills straight up, at which point they can easily poke the handler's skin. I asked Marnie to fetch me a small towel to wrap Harlow in until he relaxed, and then I ran a series of blood tests to put them at ease.

"Is it rabies?" Gerry asked with urgency. "I've heard that dogs foam at the mouth when they have rabies. Do you think Harlow has rabies? Should we be getting rabies shots if we've been exposed?" Gerry wrung his hands and paced around the examination room. He turned to his partner, Kurt. "Was Harlow vaccinated?"

"Well, actually—" I said.

"I know what it is," he interrupted. "It's that Lyme disease, isn't it?"

"Gerry," Kurt said calmly, "let the woman talk."

"But, honey, they say that this is the worst area for Lyme disease, and there's deer ticks everywhere. Two people at the office came down with it last summer. And remember when that popular little girl singer that we like, the one who wears all the black eyeliner—Avril Lavigne—got it? Horrible, horrible disease."

Gerry was an emotional runaway train, so I simply got out of his way and took Harlow with me. I scooped up the small brown-and-white hedgehog before he could curl into a tight ball and roll right off the exam table. Harlow seemed a peculiar pet choice for Gerry and Kurt. Native to Africa and also the United Kingdom, hedgehogs tend to be shy creatures that recoil from loud noise, preferring quiet and dimly lit environments. Yet as I stroked Harlow's sugar white, soft underbelly fur, he slowly let out a carefree purr, indicating that he was completely at ease—even with Gerry, whose personality was nothing less than bright, big, and booming.

"Gerry," Kurt said, holding steady. "Let Dr. Hess look at Harlow and tell us what's wrong. That's why we're here, remember?"

"Yes, of course, you're right." Gerry turned to me with intensity. But just as I was about to reassure him that Harlow did not have Lyme disease, he jumped back in, asking, "Isn't Connecticut the worst place for Lyme disease? They even named a town after it."

"That's why it's called Lyme disease, Gerry. It originated there."

"Oh, my God, that's it." Gerry put his hands up to his neck. "What if Harlow gave it to us?" He began pressing his skin. "My glands feel a little bit swollen."

Kurt took a deep breath. "You don't have Lyme."

If I allowed them to, Gerry and Kurt would volley back and forth like this forever. I tapped on the computer screen to bring up Harlow's blood panel to show Gerry.

"Look at this." I pointed at the reading. "Harlow's negative for Lyme." I knew that would be the result before I'd even run the test because hedgehogs rarely, if ever, get Lyme disease. To my knowledge, there's only been one reported case ever in a hedgehog, and that animal lived primarily outdoors.

Gerry was nonplussed. "But all that foamy saliva," he sputtered. "That can't be healthy. Is it rabies, then?"

We were back to rabies. Kurt looked up at me with a defeated shrug.

"Harlow does not have Lyme or rabies. In fact, he's a very healthy little guy. Harlow is exhibiting a normal behavior for hedgehogs. It's called self-anointing."

Gerry knit his brow. "Self what?"

"Hedgehogs have a keen sense of smell, and when they encounter a new scent, especially if it's something new in their environment, they will lick the object until they form a sort of 'spit ball' that they use to cover themselves." I pointed to Harlow's back. "That's the foamy lather you see."

Gerry made a face of distaste. "And this is normal?"

"Completely normal. Can you think of anything new with an unusual or unfamiliar smell that you've introduced into his environment lately?"

Kurt shot Gerry a look. "It's the spritzer."

"Oh, no you don't," Gerry dismissed him. "And please, it's called cologne."

Kurt turned to me, "He's been wearing a new 'cologne.'"

"Guile—from Barneys." Gerry added. "It smells like vanilla, mint, and lavender."

"And Harlow wasn't foaming up at all before you started wearing it," Kurt offered.

Gerry rolled his eyes.

I couldn't help but smile at their niggling exchange. Gerry folded his arms. "What's funny, Doctor?"

"It smells lovely, but if Kurt's right and Harlow didn't start foaming up until it was introduced into the home, then—"

"You need to stop wearing it," Kurt finished my sentence.

"Yes." I nodded in agreement. "This is my best medical advice."

Gerry threw his hands up in defeat, and Kurt sweetly took one of them in his own. "What have I been telling you? You smell better without it."

Gerry blushed and shook him off. "Oh, stop. Don't be dirty in front of the baby."

He carefully picked Harlow up off the examination table.

"Come to Daddy," he whispered. Harlow relaxed his prickly spines, and Gerry cuddled him affectionately. For the first time since he'd walked into the exam room, Gerry let out a deep exhale.

12:00 P.M., SUGAR BUDDIES' "CORPORATE OFFICE"

I ONCE PARTICIPATED in a sting operation with a licensed reptile rehabilitator and the Southern Westchester County Police Department. We seized more than one hundred illegal reptiles, including rare species of tortoises and giant snakes, from an abandoned warehouse where the breeder had set up shop. He'd gone out of town and entrusted the care of the animals to one of his employees, who had decided to take the money and run. For two weeks, the poor animals had been left unfed and baking in cages under heat lamps in a badly ventilated warehouse in the middle of July.

It was like something out of *Law & Order: Reptile Division*. The warehouse smelled so bad from rotting flesh that we had to wear gas masks to retrieve the animals. Many of them had died, and those still alive were badly burned and dehydrated by the time we arrived. We carefully transported them from the warehouse to the animal hospital, where I could rehydrate them and treat their wounds, but it was months before the survivors had recovered enough to be adopted or transferred to a rescue organization. I'd heard stories of illegal reptile brokers in the past, but I had never imagined anything as horrific as what I saw that night.

This experience reinforced my commitment to advise clients to purchase any exotic animal from a reputable breeder or to adopt it from a responsible source. A breeder's practices, including how the animal is housed and fed and what other animals it is exposed to, can determine the health of any animal, so I only refer clients to breeders with reputations for being careful and meticulous or who display and sell animals at reputable pet shows, where the clients can not only buy a new pet but also acquire all the accouterments—cage, light, heater, bedding, and food—that the animal requires.

As Elliot and I drove down a long gravel driveway toward the address entered in our GPS, I shuddered at the memory of all those abused reptiles and braced myself for whatever we might find. But as we made one last turn, the farm setting was so beautiful that I wondered if the map had led us astray. Had we taken a wrong turn? On one side of the road, an orchard of dormant apple trees extended their crooked limbs in silent greeting. On the other, an expansive pasture stretched out to a frozen pond. Ahead, a barn that slanted slightly to the side stood in front of a grove of tall pine trees, all dusted in snow. Red roosters and hens flocked together, pecking at a patch of feed just outside the big barn doors, and a potbellied pig lumbered around the side. He looked up and grunted in our direction as we drew closer.

"Well, this is picturesque," I said to Elliot.

Any sickness breeding here wasn't apparent on the surface. I pulled into the dirt parking lot and cut the engine just as the figure of a man emerged from an adjacent nineteenth-century farmhouse.

"Hello," I called as I got out of the car. I suddenly felt silly wearing my white lab coat over my jeans and riding boots. Elliot had talked me into it on the drive out from the mall.

"Makes you look official," he had encouraged me. "You know, like a real doctor."

I cast him a sideways look. "I *am* a real doctor. But I know what you mean. I'll put it on."

Dressed in denim jeans and a woolly, cranberry sweater, the man walked comfortably toward us across the parking lot.

"Good morning, I'm Simon Daniels," he said, extending his hand. "Awfully cold for a farm tour, isn't it?" he grinned, looking a bit like Hugh Grant and not at all like the suspicious breeder type.

I took his hand and shook it. "I'm Dr. Laurie Hess of the Veterinary Center for Birds & Exotics in Bedford Hills, and this is my intern, Elliot."

"Ah, yes, in Westchester County. I've heard of it," he said and nodded warmly at Elliot. "What can I do you for?"

Simon's easy charm disarmed me, and I paused, but then I forced an image of Mathilda lying listless at the bottom of her cage. We were here for her and Lily. "We understand you breed sugar gliders?"

"I do," he said without hesitation as his grin returned. "This farm has been in my family for two generations. My father and my father's father. Breeding animals is about all I know how to do." He laughed easily at himself.

"And you sell your gliders as well?"

"I do that too, although I don't sell them here." He cocked his head to the side. "You interested in buying gliders, Doctor?"

"No." I paused. "But I think I've treated a few of yours that were sold at the mall—Johnson Valley?"

"Yes, I have a Sugar Buddies kiosk there. Many of my babies were recently adopted from that location." Simon beamed. "Lots of people scooped them up for holiday gifts."

Elliot and I exchanged a regretful look.

"Is something wrong?" Simon stopped. "Did you say you recently 'treated' some of my gliders?"

"At least two gliders from Johnson Valley Mall arrived at my hospital very sick. I've treated three others who might have come from there too." I cleared my throat. "All but one has died."

"What?" he took a disarming step back.

"From what appears to be malnutrition," I continued. "Their seizures and tremors were textbook—very common in gliders with diets low in calcium, vitamin D, and protein—but I ran blood tests on every single one of them. I studied their X-rays, and it's not malnutrition. Something else is making them sick. Very sick."

"Wait a minute, wait a minute." Simon said. "Slow down. My gliders are dying? I don't understand."

"We don't, either. That's why we're here." I paused and looked around the yard.

Simon followed my gaze. "I hope you don't think they're dying because of something we're doing here at the farm?"

That had been my hunch. But now I wasn't so sure. Of course I'd only just met him, but I sensed that Simon was one of the good guys, a responsible and trustworthy breeder. And yet he'd just confirmed my lead that the gliders sold at Johnson Valley Mall had come directly from his farm. Though this didn't explain the spread of the sickness throughout the country, there was no denying that I'd just made a solid link between at least two of the sick gliders admitted to my hospital—Pockets and Mathilda.

"One of your gliders recently purchased at Johnson Valley Mall is very possibly dying at my animal hospital right now," I said, "and I cannot treat her until I know what is making her sick. So I'm here, just looking for answers and for some help. I don't want to lose another animal, sir."

"I don't either," Simon agreed.

"So, if you're saying that the gliders purchased from Johnson Valley Mall came directly from your farm, can you think of anything that could be making them sick? Like, have you altered their diets? Changed cleaning supplies?" I nervously rattled off every possibility I'd thought of. "Have you intro-. duced any new breeders to the group? Hired new staff? Any recent building construction?"

Simon shook his head back and forth as I suggested anything and everything I could think of that might contribute to the mysterious sickness.

"Doctor, I assure you," he said when I was finally finished, "conditions here are clean and safe. I don't create risk or leave anything to chance."

"I believe you," I hedged, "but—"

Again Simon followed my eyes as I looked around the grounds. Elliot tightened his scarf as a flock of crows stirred in the trees nearby. Simon broke the silence and my uncertainty about what to do next.

"I understand," he said, straightening up. "Seeing is believing, right? My glider barn is over there." He pointed across the lot. "We're gonna freeze out here, so let me show you inside. Then you can see for yourself."

As we walked across the parking lot, Simon wondered aloud, "Have you spoken to the gliders' owners? These aren't low-maintenance animals, as I'm sure you know, Doctor. They can be easily stressed. If they're not properly nourished and hydrated, sugar gliders will become weak, fatigued, and dehydrated—just as you've described."

"I know, and that's what I assumed at first too, but from what I can tell, the animals were receiving proper care in their new homes. Their owners were doing everything they were instructed to do," I said.

I can tell almost instantly when an owner isn't following instructions for proper care. My mind flipped back to Kira, the owner of a sugar glider whom I'd treated several years ago.

"Sammy can't survive on just fruit," I'd said to Kira. She was holding her emaciated glider in the palm of her hand. "Sammy needs protein—either in pellet form or by feeding him insects."

"Bugs are gross," Kira sneered.

I expected this reaction from children, but Kira was an adult—or a young adult, anyway. I took a leveling breath and smiled. "I'm not a huge fan of bugs either, but sugar gliders are omnivores—insects are a large portion of their diet in their natural habitat."

"I'm a vegan, though."

"Okay," I said as lightly as I could. "Let's try to compromise. You want Sammy to live a good long life, don't you?"

"Well, duh." Kira shrugged.

"Of course you do. But if you insist on Sammy being a vegan, too, he won't survive. If you had a baby and that baby needed milk to survive—what would you do?"

"I'm only nineteen. I'm not even *thinking* about having babies right now."

This was a relief to hear, but she was missing my point. I rephrased the question. "At some point—in the distant future— if your baby needed something, wouldn't you give it to him?"

She rolled her eyes. "I'm not going to be a bad mother if that's what you're saying."

"Exactly, you'd give him what he needs. And right now Sammy needs protein, so let's discuss some ways you can get him what he needs without it grossing you out."

SIMON UNLOCKED THE double doors to a long, narrow wooden barn with a low, angled metal roof that would provide seasonal protection from harsh sun, rain, and snow and also keep out predators such as hawks, snakes, coyotes, and foxes. It was forty degrees outside, but in Simon's glider den, the atmosphere was warm and cozy. I guessed it was upward of eighty degrees. Sugar gliders have very little fur when they're first born, so they have a difficult time regulating their own body temperature. Climate control for newborns is essential.

Simon tossed a look back at Elliot. "Might want to lose the scarf, buddy. It's summertime in here."

The gliders were stacked in rows of individual wire cages, each with its own light source to provide warmth. There must have been three hundred cages in there. Maybe more. A few workers wearing clean brown coveralls buzzed around the barn like bees in a hive, cleaning cages and offering gliders heaping bowls of pelleted food and produce. Shallow tubs of bleach diluted in water—footbaths to limit the spread of any potential infection—sat at the entrance of the barn for anyone who entered.

"Slip on a pair"—Simon gestured toward a heap of rubber boots—"and I'll show you around."

Elliot and I pulled the oversized boots over our shoes.

"Mamas and their babies on the right," Simon explained. "Gliders just out of the pouch on the left."

Like other marsupials, such as kangaroos, wallabies, and koala bears, sugar gliders give birth to relatively undeveloped babies. The young gliders crawl out of their mother's belly when they're no bigger than the size of a pea and head straight for her snuggly and safe protective pouch, where they spend nearly two months nursing before they're large enough to wean and actually be "born."

I bent forward and peered inside a cage. Five or six gliders were nestled together in a bed of shredded newspaper. The baby on top of the heap cracked open a curious, bright eye.

"How old are these little ones?" I whispered, trying not to disturb them.

"They just crawled out of Mama's pouch maybe three days ago. We won't sell them until they can easily eat on their own. That'll take a month at least."

"Look at those little pink toes," I said, warming to the sweet scene. "And those teeny-tiny ears. It's amazing how small they are."

Simon held up a thumb and said, "And hardly this long when I send them out."

I pointed to another baby curled up in the corner of the cage. "Look at that one—you can just start to see a charcoal stripe growing in down his back."

I broke away from Simon and Elliot and walked down a row of wire cages. The floor was completely free of debris, and each cage was neat and tidy. Given the hundreds, if not thousands, of animals that Simon was housing here, the level of cleanliness was impressive. Large fans whirred near the ceiling and kept the room well ventilated. I didn't detect even a whiff of urine or feces. There was no smell of any harsh chemicals either, remarkable considering the number of cleaning products that would be necessary to achieve this level of disinfection. Harsh chemicals or excessive ammonia buildup from urine could damage the gliders' respiratory tracts and make them more vulnerable to infection, which I had considered as a possible source of illness. But now, as I walked up and down the meticulously kept rows of cages, I had to rule that out too.

Simon walked up behind me. "So to answer your questions—all my glider cages are cleaned routinely, and the animals are given fresh food and water twice daily. We haven't added any new supplements or changed their food recently. No new cleaning supplies, new hires, or construction anywhere on site either. I use the same breeding stock from year to year, and all of my breeders are checked regularly to make sure the animals are healthy. The protocol here is that any gliders exhibiting the slightest signs of sickness are removed from the group, isolated, and treated until they're healthy enough to rejoin the others. I haven't treated a sick glider in months, if not longer."

"The animals all look healthy; they don't appear to be lacking in anything."

"I'd say 'I told you so.'"

I stopped and turned toward Simon. "I didn't mean to offend you by suggesting otherwise," I explained, "but I'm sure you understand why I wanted to see for myself."

Simon nodded.

"With your permission, I'd like to take one of the babies back with me to the hospital to run some general blood tests and perform a stool examination. I promise to personally provide the animal with proper nutrition and excellent care."

Simon thought about it for a moment. "It's an unusual request, but if you think it'll help . . . "

"I hope it will help me rule out your farm as the source of infection or point me in another direction if I pick up any abnormalities in the young glider's test results."

"And assuming the tests come back clean, what do we do next?"

"We?"

He motioned toward the rows of cages. "Doctor, I'm just as concerned as you that any of my gliders are dying. This isn't just a business for me. I care about these animals—they're my babies. If something's making them sick, I need to do something about it. And the sooner the better. My next shipment is scheduled to go out tomorrow."

"Where's it going?"

"Trucks to Long Island and Chicago are set to leave in the morning."

"Chicago?" I felt a prickly sense of foreboding. Hadn't the *Westchester Journal* article explicitly said that Sugar Buddies sold exotic animals at malls throughout the tristate area?

"Do you sell your gliders in other areas outside the Northeast?"

"Well, I don't, but Exotic Essentials does."

The name put me on alert. Something was starting to click into place. "And what is Exotic Essentials?"

"They're my chief distributor."

Simon must have recognized my puzzled expression. He explained, "I breed hundreds of sugar gliders at one time, and then Exotic Essentials buys them from me and distributes them to local kiosks like Sugar Buddies in malls all over the country."

Click.

"Do you know which states specifically?"

"Jeez, all over. Massachusetts, Connecticut—"

"Tampa?" I asked, although, to my regret, I already knew the answer.

His eyes widened. "Are gliders turning up sick in Tampa too?"

"Gliders are turning up dead all over the country."

2:05 P.M., SUGAR BUDDIES' "CORPORATE OFFICE"

MY MIND WAS buzzing as Elliot and I got back into the car.

"No cell service out here," I groaned and tapped at my phone repeatedly.

I was in a rush to call Hannah, my colleague and former mentor from the Animal Medical Center in Manhattan who now had an exotic animal practice in Long Island similar to mine. Simon had confirmed that a shipment of nearly two dozen gliders would be arriving at the Winslow Mall tomorrow, not twenty miles from Hannah's clinic. If any of them became sick, Hannah would likely be the first to treat them. She needed to know everything I'd recently learned about the fast-spreading sickness.

As I turned onto the main road, my Android phone emitted a series of dings.

"Cell service," I cheered and quickly entered my passcode. Eight missed calls. Oh, no. I drew in a worried breath, assuming the calls had come from the hospital. Had Mathilda's condition further declined? Had another sick glider been brought in? When I scanned the call list, I saw that none of the calls were from Marnie; rather, two were from Luke's school, and the rest were from Peter. My professional concern shifted to maternal worry. I quickly called Peter's cell, and Luke picked up.

"Hi, Mom!" he chirped. "I'm using Dad's cell phone."

He was okay. Or at least he sounded okay.

"Luke, honey, are you hurt? Why did your school call me? Did something happen?"

Believe it or not, at ten years old, Luke's almost taller than I am, but he'll always be my baby.

"I'm fine. The nurse just says I have the pink eyes."

I exhaled and smiled at the malapropism. Pink "eyes" I could handle. "Honey, remember you've had this before. The two most important things—wash your hands, and don't touch your eyes. Pink eye is highly contagious."

"I know," he grumbled. "That's what Dad said."

"Did Dad pick you up from school?"

"Yeah, about fifteen minutes ago."

It took me a few seconds to put it all together. The school had called me, but I hadn't been able to receive the calls at Simon's farm. After trying me twice, they'd called Peter, and he'd come to the rescue. He must have canceled his late-afternoon conference call in the city in order to pick up Luke. I squirmed, feeling bad that I'd been out of touch. I'd missed another maternal moment, and as he so often and dependably does, Peter had shown up in my absence. I was sure he'd done it without hesitation or any resentment toward me, and still I wished that I'd been there instead.

"Where is Dad now, and why do you have his cell phone?"

"He's inside the drug store getting my subscription."

"Prescription," I gently corrected him.

"You know what I mean," he sighed. I imagined him flipping back his tangle of strawberry curls.

"Have him call me, okay? Once Brett's done with soccer practice, I'll be home as soon as I can."

"Mom?" his voice sweetened. "Can I order Chinese from GrubHub?"

"No, Luke, you don't need food delivery. You've got your father to fix you a snack. I'll be home soon, okay?"

And with that, his adolescent tone returned. "Okayyyyy."

I hung up and quietly stared out at the snow-covered road ahead.

After a few quiet moments, Elliot said, "My mom's always been a bookkeeper. I bet your boys think you have the coolest job in the world."

He'd overheard enough, I guessed, to pick up on my perpetual mommy guilt.

"Yeah," I said, attempting to smile as I stared ahead. "I guess they think it's pretty cool."

I thought back to the time I'd brought four Flemish giant rabbits and a dozen baby chicks to Luke's class before the Easter holiday. As I spread them out on the lawn so his classmates could pet and chase them around, I overheard Luke, a first grader then, bragging to a group of his friends, "That's my mom. She's an animal doctor."

But that was just one special day many years ago. What about all of the others?

3:30 P.M., ANIMAL HOSPITAL

ELLIOT AND I walked through the glass double doors right behind Alan, the FedEx guy.

"Delivery!" he chirped.

"More bird food?" I teased.

This was our running joke. Alan had been delivering to the hospital since nearly the day we opened, and though he was good-humored now, in the beginning "more bird food" was his constant complaint. Back then, he'd arrive with a delivery—carts piled high with hay, dollies stacked with cumbersome equipment, and heavy bags of bird food that he'd haul in haughtily on his shoulders. One afternoon he struggled through the waiting room trying to negotiate an extraordinarily large bag that was punctured and spilling pellet all over the floor.

"Next time, I'm going to just back the truck through the front doors," he said, cursing under his breath.

"Hey, Alan," Marnie said cheerfully. "How's your day?"

"How does it look?" Alan shot back. "It's all over the floor. And every week the shipment gets heavier." He stopped to wipe the sweat off his forehead.

"I thought you might be interested in another shipment the hospital just received."

"What's that?" Alan said without breaking his concentration on the floor. "Because I'm almost done here."

"Four rescued degus. We're looking to find them new homes."

Alan stopped chasing the last of the stray pellets on the floor and squinted up at Marnie.

With their brown fur and long tails, these small South American rodents look like oversized gerbils; though often as large as rats, they are much more cuddly and approachable. They're playful, curious, and quick, and they love to climb and dart around.

"Want to take a look?" Marnie smiled. Without his realizing it, Marnie had gleaned something about Alan. She had observed that nearly every time he made a delivery, he'd stop in the lobby to peer over his glasses at our collage of animal photos. In particular, he'd pause at the image of a family of degus.

"They're pretty cute," she said, coaxing him. "Especially the little brown one that squeaks. I've nicknamed him Alan."

"Huh? You're kidding," Alan said, embarrassed. "You didn't name an animal after me."

"I did."

When Alan saw the four rescues, Marnie watched him transform from a hardened, overworked man into a young boy who'd probably always wanted a light and easy, sweet-natured pet of his own. And when Alan held the smallest of the litter in his burly hands, the rodent happily ran up his arm and perched atop his shoulder. That was the day that Alan the delivery guy took home Alan the degu.

Today Alan was whistling as he unloaded the last box from his cart when Marnie entered the waiting room.

"Finally," she said, struggling to pull her scrub top over her head.

"Who—me?" Alan asked.

"No—them." Marnie pointed at Elliot and me.

"What happened to you?" I looked her up and down. "Is that vomit?"

"Things got a little ugly around here," she said, "but the ferret in exam room three no longer has a Barbie doll head stuck in his throat."

I suppressed a smile. "And what about our patient in ICU?" My heart sank again when I thought about Mathilda.

Marnie shook her head. "Motionless. Still not eating. Won't even take food from the syringe when I try to feed her."

I held up the small cage. Simon had carefully removed a baby glider from a new litter and packed him up for transport to the hospital. "I brought this one back from the farm. Elliot's calling him Baby G." The tiny baby glider was curled up in my purple chenille scarf in one corner of the cage. Simon hadn't had more than shredded newspaper to keep the baby insulated once we left the warmth of the glider barn, so I'd wrapped him in my scarf to nest in.

"Let's run a series of general blood tests and get a stool sample on this little one. I want to monitor him closely. If he begins to show even the slightest sign of sickness, let me know. If he remains healthy, well then, it's much less likely that the farm is the source of illness." Less likely, I thought, but still possible.

I LEFT MARNIE with Baby G and walked back to my office. I closed the door and dialed Hannah's number at her clinic in Long Island.

"Laurie," she answered after the first ring. "To what do I owe the pleasure?"

"I wish this were just a friendly catch-up call."

I started at the beginning, recounting how each of the four gliders admitted to my hospital in the past two weeks had gotten sick and died. I described Mathilda's deteriorating condition and Lily's less severe but similar symptoms. I concluded with my inspection of Simon's farm.

"Conditions are clean, and the gliders all appear healthy," I said. "But a new shipment of gliders goes on sale at Winslow Mall tomorrow. I'm really praying that another doesn't become sick."

Hannah said. "If the breeder knows they're getting sick, why doesn't he hold off on the shipment?"

"He doesn't have room for them. He's housing hundreds of gliders at a time. And he's convinced they're leaving his farm healthy. Says he checks every animal for parasites, diarrhea, or any other sign of infection the day they ship. If there's any question they're sick, he doesn't put them on the truck."

"So then are they getting sick in transport?" Hannah was asking me the same progression of questions I'd asked Simon before heading back to the hospital.

"He doesn't think that's it, either. According to the vendors, they're arriving at the malls in good health."

"But there's some connection between his pet gliders and all the deaths?" Hannah asked.

"There seems to be." I ran my hand through my hair. I just didn't know what it was.

"Okay," said Hannah. "Send me the blood test results and films of all the gliders that have gotten sick, including Lily's and Mathilda's, and I'll take a fresh look."

"I really appreciate it. Call me tomorrow?"

"You bet," she assured me. "As soon as I know anything."

4

MEET ME IN THE MIDDLE

THURSDAY, 10:00 A.M., ANIMAL HOSPITAL

"As you can see, Pinky is a bit more than we bargained for," said Jim as he let his six-foot-long Nile monitor out of an extra-large gym bag.

Wearing a pressed plaid button-down shirt and crisp Dockers, Jim was handling his pet reptile with yellow oven mitts. As soon as he set the big lizard down on the floor, the animal began to thrash about, whipping his tail left and right and extending his long reptilian tongue nearly a foot in every direction. His sharp claws raked across the tile floor. Despite his energy and size, he didn't look healthy; his skin had peeled in many places, and his coloring looked off.

Many species of lizards make popular pets. Iguanas are probably the most popular of the larger lizards because they bond closely with their owners. Nile monitors, on the other hand, tend to be quite feisty and formidable creatures, and, in all honesty, they don't make the best pets. They're aggressive, strong, and not at all shy about using their powerful bite. In order to manage pet owners' expectations about how their interactions will go with a Nile monitor as it gets older, I've been known to say, "If you're going to bring home a Nile monitor, be sure to have a first aid kit at hand."

I'd expected Pinky to be grumpy, but I hadn't been prepared for him to be so big. Nile monitors can grow as long as seven feet, but I'd never seen one this big in captivity. Pinky was the size of a small alligator.

"I promise you," Jim's girlfriend, Becky, said, giggling nervously, "he wasn't even *half* this size when we bought him."

She backed away just as Pinky's three-foot-long tail whipped around in her direction.

"He was just the cutest little thing running up and down my arm." She made a flitting motion with her fingertips on her white cashmere cardigan.

Because this was my first introduction to Pinky, I stood back initially. His owners were sure to be more familiar with their reptile's particular moods than I was, so I watched as Jim attempted to corner the animal and pick him up off the floor. He squatted down low and extended his oven-mitt-clad hands as he attempted to back Pinky against a wall. Pinky hissed and lunged away from him. When Jim tried again unsuccessfully, I buzzed Marnie to assist me. We needed all hands—and mitts—on deck with this one.

"We both had gargoyle geckos as first pets," Becky explained. "I guess you could say we're natural lizard lovers." She smiled adoringly in Jim's direction.

Though gargoyle geckos and Nile monitors are both in the lizard family, they're worlds apart. Gargoyle geckos are found on the island of New Caledonia, near Australia. Nile monitors are found in Africa. In disposition, they're even further removed. Geckos are gentle little lizards that I recommend as first pets for small children because they're low maintenance and easygoing. Nile monitors are not at all beginner reptiles. They can be obstinate and sometimes dangerous, and they're almost always big. They really don't belong in a traditional home unless the owners are very experienced reptile handlers. I imagined Jim and Becky at their local pet store, unknowingly selecting Pinky from a tank of young Nile monitors.

"They didn't look this large in the pictures," she said, making conversation.

I guessed that Becky was referring to the colorful booklet pet stores often provide with purchase, titled something like "Your Nile Monitor and You." I'd seen my share of those free handouts—full of glossy color photographs but light on relevant information. "Your Nile Monitor and You" probably didn't mention the room-sized enclosure Jim and Becky would need once Pinky reached his full size, which they would need to outfit with branches for him to climb, large rocks on which he could rub off shedding skin, a shallow pool for bathing, climate control, and UV light exposure for ten to twelve hours a day. This reptile was high maintenance.

Jim finally managed to grab Pinky firmly behind the neck and wrangle him into his arms. Becky cooed, "Our baby."

Except that Pinky could no longer be held like a baby. Jim was struggling to keep the large animal from wriggling out of his grip. Beads of sweat formed on his upper lip and at his hairline. Pinky whipped his tail and jerked his head from side to side.

"Can you, um, grasp the middle?" he asked me desperately.

Together, Jim and I carried Pinky over to the examination table just as Marnie entered the room with a large blanket. I secured Pinky by covering him in the blanket and rolling him up like a fifty-pound burrito.

"He's a live one," Marnie said under her breath. "Reminds me of Tybalt."

"Let's hope for a different outcome," I whispered back.

Tybalt, a seven-foot-long iguana, had become a legend at the hospital the day he wriggled out of my arms and vaulted off the X-ray table, and—*snap!*—two entire feet of his bright green tail fell right off. The broken half skittered to the floor and slid under the examination table.

"Grab his body!" I'd screamed at Marnie. "I'll get the tail!"

In general, lizards should be handled gently and held under the body when picked up. They should never be picked up by their tails because, as we'd just experienced, the tail can break off. More accurately, their tails don't really break; they detach from the body. Referred to as "tail autonomy," it's a common defense mechanism for many lizards. If they feel especially threatened, they will distract a predator by detaching their tail. The separated tail thrashes and wiggles about, increasing the lizard's chances of escaping to safety. I'd seen geckos perform this trick time and again, but never an iguana the size of Tybalt. Whereas the smaller gecko's tail grows back fairly quickly, I feared it would be years before Tybalt's grew back, if at all, and even then it would likely be an entirely different color from the rest of his body. I couldn't help but think of one of Brett's favorite childhood books, *The Mixed-Up Chameleon* by Eric Carle, in which a chameleon wishes to be like other animals in the zoo and ends up with the head of an elephant, the neck of a giraffe, and the tail of a fox. I could only guess what Tybalt might look like should his tail ever return.

"HE'S STARTING TO settle," I said to Jim and Becky. "I'm going to remove the blanket now." I readjusted my grip and carefully examined the areas of skin Pinky hadn't shed yet. I noted that his skin was an orange-brown color, not the bright green it should have been. This color change could stem from a number of factors: inappropriate diet, the wrong environmental temperature, not enough UV light.

Whenever I examine an animal whose behavior or health status has changed abruptly, I ask its owners questions about any changes in the family, any recent moves or events that might have disrupted a regular routine. In veterinary school, students learn to look for the most obvious causes for a disorder before considering the more obscure possibilities. It's called differential diagnosis—moving from one possible cause to another, taking into account all of the animal's symptoms. The saying "When you hear hoofbeats, think horses, not zebras" reminds us veterinarians not to discount the obvious when looking for the cause of a problem—although, as an exotic animal vet, I am inclined to think about zebras before horses.

"Has anything changed lately with his care?" I asked.

"He recently outgrew his tank," Jim said, "so we converted the guest room."

"Jim completely transformed it," Becky said, beaming, "with peat moss and a bunch of plants from Lowe's. He even bought one of those long metal tubs people plant tomatoes in. Pinky uses it as a bathtub." I briefly imagined the guest room in my own house converted into a tropical wonderland. It sounded kind of magical, except—

"Except"—Jim sighed—"now that he's out of his climate-controlled tank, we have to crank the central heating throughout the entire house to keep him warm enough. It's like a sauna."

Becky giggled again. "More like a hot yoga class."

Just thinking about the heat seemed to elevate Jim's body temperature. He wiped another bead of sweat from his upper lip.

When it comes to exotic pets—feathered, furry, or scaly—the temperature of their world is often critical, so providing the proper climate to help keep the animal healthy is paramount. Perhaps more than any other type of pet, reptiles have specific temperature needs and requirements. Most captive lizards require enclosures with a warm basking zone, often in the range of ninety to one hundred degrees. This often means adding supplemental heating elements such as heat bulbs and heating pads to enclosures when seasonal temperatures fall and removing them when they climb again. If Jim and Becky were turning up the household thermostat to match this level of heat, Pinky was probably comfortable, but they were likely roasting.

"And our heating bill is astronomical."

Becky chimed in, "The heat we can get used to, but"—she looked over at Jim—"now that we no longer have a guest room, we're not sure where to put my parents."

"They'll be visiting from Santa Fe for the holidays," Jim explained.

"Well, then they'll be used to the heat," I joked. "Are your parents reptile lovers like you? New Mexico sure has its fair share of them."

Becky and Jim exchanged looks of concern.

"Not really," Becky said slowly. "They're more like . . . cat people."

"Ah," I said, understanding. "They like animals that cuddle up on your lap?"

Becky nodded just as Pinky broke loose from the grip I had around his throat. I reached toward him, and he lunged at my hand—his way of warning me that he no longer wanted to be restrained, or probably held at all. "Well, if that's the case," I said, sizing up the frightened lizard, "then Pinky may come as a bit of a surprise. Have you considered putting them up in your nearest Comfort Inn?"

AFTER JIM AND Becky had left with Pinky and my general recommendation to give him a few more weeks to adjust to his new room, Marnie and I huddled in the hallway.

"How's Luke today?" she asked.

"Quarantined. He officially has pinkeye."

"Oh, no," said Marnie, wincing in sympathy.

"Don't feel too bad. He's home from school today with the house to himself. He couldn't be happier."

Luke may be the younger of my two boys, but he's definitely the more independent. He's content to be alone and will figure things out in the absence of my or Peter's help. I'd left him camped out in his room with his canaries Lennon and Ringo. I imagined that he was probably now playing online chess or practicing his piano undisturbed, aside from the occasional bird song. Luke has always had an ear for music. By his choice, he started to play the piano and take voice lessons at the age of five. For his eighth birthday he asked for a pet bird, so I got him a male canary since they sing so beautifully. Luke named him Lennon because he has a ring of feathers around his head that Luke insists look "just like the

Beatles' bangs." A year later, he asked for a companion for his singing canary because, "Duh, Mom, Lennon needs a buddy." So along came Ringo, who perfectly accompanies Lennon's vocals and Luke's piano chords.

"Still, you know how it goes—one person gets it, and the whole house goes down. My daughter caught it last winter, and it was only a matter of days until the boys had it, too."

My neighbor Katherine had said nearly the same thing to me this morning when I walked Brett down the driveway to catch the bus. He'd asked me not to, but I'd insisted. "I just want two extra minutes with my oldest son, okay?"

Katherine was standing alongside Gilman, who acted equally embarrassed to have a mom escort. The boys greeted each other, mumbling, "Hey, man," and quickly followed each other onto the bus.

As Katherine and I walked back toward our homes, she said with artificial concern, "How is Luke? Is he staying home today with pinkeye?"

How did she know Luke had pinkeye?

"Gilman told me that Peter picked him up from school yesterday. Conjunctivitis is so highly contagious, as I'm sure you know since you're a doctor. I was relieved to hear that your husband was right there to bring him home."

"That's Peter," I said, attempting to smile. "The dependable one."

I returned my attention to Marnie. "I'll bring home a box of latex 'kid' gloves to keep the germs at bay." I nodded toward the ICU. "One sick ward is enough."

Just then the front doors to the hospital swung open, bringing in a rush of cold air. A woman in dark sunglasses and a belted winter trench coat charged in.

"Who's that?" muttered Marnie.

I took a guess. "Jeanne, Bob's wife."

The woman took off her glasses to reveal seemingly permanently arched eyebrows. She was striking in a beautiful but hardened way. Her eyes scanned the waiting room, and when she spotted me at the far end, she demanded, "Where is he?"

By "he," I assumed she was speaking about Bob.

"He just left," I said calmly, keeping my voice neutral.

She'd missed him by less than an hour. Bob had been my first client of the day before Jim and Becky. He was here right at nine, as had become his new morning routine, appearing with hot coffee for Marnie and me soon after we opened.

"My way of thanking you for all the extra care you're giving my girls," he said apologetically.

If anyone should apologize, I thought, it's me. I wished Mathilda and Lily were responding to our treatments and showing signs of improvement, but neither of Bob's gliders, especially Mathilda, was improving. Her young and fragile organs were losing their functionality. We were continuing to pump fluids under her skin to keep her hydrated, but she had stopped producing urine and was dangerously dehydrated. Ideally, we'd have placed an intravenous catheter in her leg to deliver fluids directly into her veins, as we do with many exotic pets, but her veins were just too tiny to thread a catheter into. There wasn't much more we could do.

"I think it's time we move Mathilda to an isolation ward," I said regretfully.

"Move her?" Bob said distressed. "Why can't they stay together?"

"I'd love to keep them together, but to prevent further spread of illness, I really need to separate them. This will give Lily a greater chance of survival."

"And what about Mathilda? Will she—survive?"

I held back. There was no doubt in my mind she was dying, and she was likely in pain. At this point, I'd normally suggest euthanizing the animal. But sometimes doing what's most humane for the pet is the most difficult decision for the owner to make. I looked into Bob's sad eyes and realized that I, too, was hoping beyond reason that Mathilda would miraculously revive or that I'd finally find a way to save her before I lost her too.

Jeanne was positioned in the middle of the waiting room with her hands on her hips and her black pumps bolted to the ground. "I know they're sick, Doctor. Of course, Bob tells me that it's 'nothing to worry about,'" she said sarcastically, making air quotes. "But I wasn't born yesterday, you know. Just show me where they are," she said impatiently.

I hesitated and considered that Bob was my client, not Jeanne. I didn't have to answer to her. My responsibility was to *his* pets, Lily and Mathilda. Yet I couldn't really throw his wife out in the cold. As much as I didn't want to, I walked Jeanne back into the isolation ward. She gazed indifferently down at Mathilda.

"Why isn't she moving?"

"We're treating her for potential sepsis and hyporvolemia."

Jeanne regarded me coolly. "I'm not exactly sure what that means, but judging by the look of her, it sounds serious. I don't know what Bob has told you, but we cannot afford to keep any animal alive that isn't going to make it."

I regarded Jeanne from head to toe in her modish clothes and knew well that it wasn't that Bob couldn't afford it. It was that Jeanne didn't support treatment of his animals. In other words, she didn't think they were worth the expense. Before I could say a word, she turned on her high heels and left.

I retreated to my office and shut the door. My nerves were frayed. I slumped down in my swivel desk chair and stared blankly at my computer, hoping that an answer to the mystery would magically pop up on the screen. I closed my eyes in resignation. *I just need five minutes of quiet before returning to rounds.* But before I could get even that, the office phone rang. It was Simon, the glider breeder.

"Dr. Hess, I have the complete list of locations you asked for, where Exotic Essentials distributes and sells my gliders. Want me to go through them?"

"Yes, yes." I reached for the list Elliot had compiled earlier. He'd spent the morning sifting through posts on Vets Connect, listing in alphabetical order the cities and states where other veterinarians had reported sugar glider tremors, illness, and deaths.

"Go ahead," I said.

"New York, Connecticut, Massachusetts, Florida, Virginia, Illinois—"

As Simon read through the locations where his chief distributor sold his gliders, I made check marks next to the cities and states that matched up. When he finished, I scanned it from top to bottom.

I sighed and ran a hand through my hair. "They all match up."

"They all match up to what?" I could hear the nervousness in his voice.

"In every city where gliders have been reported sick or have recently died, Exotic Essentials distributes to a nearby mall."

Simon didn't say a word. In fact, he was so unresponsive that I thought we might have been disconnected.

"Simon?"

"I don't understand," he finally said. "My animals aren't showing *any* sign of sickness on the farm."

I really wanted to believe that Simon was innocent in all this, one of the good guys. But I couldn't ignore the red flags—about a dozen seemed to be pointing to his farm. Still, I found myself extending him more of my support.

"Walk me through your operation again. What happens to the gliders after they leave your farm?"

"Haven't we been through this?"

"Simon, when news of this gets out, you will be asked questions like this."

"If news of this gets out"—his voice began to quake—"I'm finished."

"Walk me through it again," I gently encouraged him.

"I pack the gliders myself into clean cages with heat rocks. This ensures that the animals stay warm, especially this time of year, when we don't want the cages to drop below eighty degrees for the babies. The gliders are separated into colonies of ten to twelve per cage, so they have ample room to move around. I provide each driver with enough food and water to last throughout the trip. The animals drink from water bottles, and their food is covered and contained to prevent the spread of germs. They don't travel more than seven or eight hours at a time, so in terms of cleaning, the cage paper can be changed as needed."

"And who drives the trucks?"

"I've been using the same transport company for a decade. In fact, the same guys have been driving these routes for years. They never leave the animals alone in the trucks or unload them until they reach their location. Just like I do, they feel personally responsible for these animals."

"Okay." I paused to think, tracking the gliders' journey from point A to point B in my head. "What happens after they arrive at the malls?"

"Their cages are directly unloaded from the trucks into the mall kiosks. It's the first and last stop the animals make before they're adopted into new homes."

"Is it possible that they're somehow becoming infected at the malls then?"

I asked the question although from everything I knew so far, the animals didn't become sick until *after* they'd been adopted and were in their new homes. I thought back to what Jackie had said at the Johnson Valley Mall information desk. She'd described the gliders as jumping and flying all over the place, active behavior characteristic of healthy gliders. Maxine, too, along with Bob and Mr. Huntington, had said similar things. Maxine recounted that Georgie's first night home had been sleepless for both her and her new pet because the young glider had bounced around, wide-eyed and energetic—exactly the type of wild night performance indicative of a healthy sugar glider.

"I can't think of anything that the vendors are doing, or not doing," Simon offered, "that would make the gliders sick, but why don't I drive down to Winslow Mall today and take a look around? Would that help?"

"It couldn't hurt."

After we hung up, I tried my colleague Hannah again. I'd already called her twice this morning, and both times my call had gone straight to voice mail. I was anxious for her interpretation of the glider films and blood test results. Had she found anything that might explain what was making the young gliders become sick? I crossed my fingers that I'd learn something today that could save Mathilda's life.

12:20 P.M.

ON THE MEDICAL record of my next patient, a macaw, Marnie had noted, "Possible broken wing."

I swung open the door to the examination room to discover the macaw's owner, Lee, precariously perched on the edge of the visitor's bench with her left leg extended. Her foot was wrapped in gauze that she'd attempted to stuff into her bright red Dansko clog.

"Just look at me," she pointed to her foot.

Lee and her five-year-old male hyacinth macaw, Bowie, were regular visitors to the animal hospital. Macaws, or New World parrots, are native to Central and South America and the Caribbean and are the largest genus of parrots, often three feet in length from head to tail, with magnificent beaks. The nineteen different species of macaws are generally named for their vibrant colors, from the red-feathered scarlet macaw, to the more common blue-and-gold macaw, to the very rare royal blue hyacinth macaw. Although the largest of the macaws, hyacinth macaws are perhaps the calmest and most even-tempered. That was definitely true of Bowie, who perched on Lee's extended leg, crunching contentedly on a macadamia nut. Whereas Bowie usually appeared tall and regal, today I noticed an obvious droop in his left wing, which hung at least four inches lower than the right one.

"Broken wing *and* broken ankle?" I asked. "Are you both injured?"

"It's that shower perch," she fussed. "It's always falling down."

Many bird owners secure a perch like Lee was describing—typically a plastic rod bent at a ninety-degree angle that suctions at one end to the tiles of the shower wall. They create the ultimate birdbath.

"What happened this time?"

"We were taking our regular morning shower together. Bowie was singing like he loves to do from his perch underneath the shower head." She leaned in toward Bowie and began to hum. "We were just singing in the rain, weren't we, darlin'?" Bowie let out a long, shrill screech, and Lee chuckled. "You're in love with your own voice, aren't you?" She began to hum again.

"And then what happened?" I gently interrupted their little moment.

"And then the suction cup on the perch came loose." She winced at the recollection. "It came right off the tile, and when I tried to catch him, I lost my balance." She looked regrettably at Bowie's wing. "He came down with me."

The key to these devices is to find one with a reliable suction cup that can hold the full weight of the bird that will use it. Bowie weighed at least five pounds, clearly too heavy for the small perch Lee was describing. No wonder Bowie had ended up at the bottom of the tub.

I reached out to Bowie. "Step up on my hand, sweetie. Let me take a look." Bowie stepped up obediently.

"Good boy." I gently wrapped a towel around his powerful back and wings, which he seemed to enjoy, although not all big birds like to be held in this way. I'd examined my share of parrots who had tried to remove my finger with their large beaks when I approached with a towel. But Bowie had no problem with being bundled up, I imagined, since he was accustomed to toweling off after his daily shower. I handed him over to Marnie so that my hands were free to examine him.

"The size of the suction cups on the perch is important," I said. "They need to be large and strong enough to support Bowie. He's a big boy." I reached underneath the towel and slowly extended Bowie's wings simultaneously to compare his strength on each side. He flinched as I did so and struggled to pull his left wing back into his body. "There is noticeable weakness on this side," I said to Lee. "We're going to need to do an X-ray." I suspected that the fall had broken the unique coracoid bone that birds have in their shoulders. "If that is the case, we'll have to bandage his wing for the next few weeks, and he'll have to rest in his cage. That also means no showers while his bandage is on, okay?"

Lee looked unhappy about the restriction but nodded in agreement.

"And you may want to consider fewer showers together in the future—fewer broken bones."

Lee frowned. "But then who will serenade me?"

"Maybe you can find another perch in the house for your duets," I said, affectionately.

I was just about to send Marnie off to take Bowie's X-ray when Elliot pushed open the door.

"Sorry to interrupt," he said anxiously, "but do you have a minute, Dr. Hess?"

I excused myself and followed him out into the hall.

"What now?"

"The media."

The television in the boarding room was replaying a news report that Elliot had recorded. A TV reporter was standing inside a mall with a jeering crowd behind him.

"They're the ultimate exotic pet," a reporter with hair smoothed perfectly into place said, "and they're up for sale at mall kiosks. But some of these tiny creatures are proving more difficult to care for than people might think. In fact, some are even turning up dead."

"Oh, no," I groaned. I backed up the video and played it again. Positioned directly behind the reporter, the sign was impossible to miss; it read "Sugar Buddies."

"When did this air?" I asked. Simon's words replayed in my mind. *If news of this gets out, I'm finished.*

"I caught it on my lunch break and recorded it right away," Elliot said. "I think there's another newscast coming up at three."

I looked at my watch. "That's in five minutes."

Marnie, Elliot, and I crowded together in the boarding room with Chloe, a mini lop-eared rabbit, who was staying with us over the winter holiday while her owner, Mr. Lombardi, was away.

"You eat lunch in here?" Marnie asked Elliot.

"It's got the biggest TV," Elliot said with a hint of embarrassment. It was true. Once I'd discovered that a little screen time calmed our overnight guests, I'd upgraded the TV. *Dora the Explorer* and *Barney & Friends* were the most popular programs for the animals; they also loved listening to Judge Judy, who was ranting from her bench right now. I looked at Chloe, who was munching on a carrot, not missing a minute of it.

MR. LOMBARDI HAD dropped Chloe off nearly two weeks before. As any rabbit owner will tell you, every rabbit has a unique personality. Some are shy and timid, while others are more playful and outgoing. All are usually somewhat skittish about being handled until they have been picked up often enough not to be afraid. Chloe was one of the most well-adjusted lop-eared rabbits I'd ever cared for, probably due to the close and loving bond she had with her owner.

"Where are you going this time?" I'd asked Mr. Lombardi, who stood tall in a black cashmere topcoat with his silver hair secured neatly in a ponytail at the nape of his neck. A world-renowned conductor, he looked like a cross between an affluent hippie and a professor. He'd taken off his lined leather gloves and was gently stroking Chloe's meticulously clean coat of fur. He moved his delicate fingers gracefully and rhythmically over Chloe's back.

"Zurich, Frankfurt, Cologne, Paris, and London . . . a few others. It's a nine-city tour," he said with a slight note of complaint.

Whereas I would have welcomed such an exciting and cultural change in scenery, Mr. Lombardi said, as he always did, that he would rather stay close at home with Chloe. I believed that he loved his rabbit more than his musical career, and each and every time the orchestra went on tour, he was clearly pained by having to leave her behind.

"It's going to be fine," I'd assured him. "I'll take excellent care of her. We love little Chloe and look forward to her stays with us."

When Mr. Lombardi didn't loosen his hold on Chloe, I knew this would be an extended good-bye. I began to prepare myself mentally for the forced extrication I'd have to perform in order to get Chloe free from his agile fingers.

"Just another minute, then I'll be on my way," he said, clutching Chloe a little closer.

"It's fine, Mr. Lombardi. Take your time," I said.

"You'll tuck her in at night?"

"Yes," I smiled. "Chloe will be safe and snug behind black-out shades and an alarm on the door."

"Can I call to check in on her?"

"Absolutely. You can check in on Chloe anytime you want. I can text you every day, too, and let you know how she is, if you'd like."

"That won't be necessary." He dismissed my offer with a wave of his hand. "I will call to check up."

Yet Mr. Lombardi never called. I think he just wanted to feel that Chloe was safe and cared for and to know that, if he needed to call, I'd answer and indulge him without question.

"Well, I guess I should be going now." He brought Chloe up close to his face and lightly touched her nose with his own. Rabbit and conductor held each other's gaze for one long, sweet moment. Then Mr. Lombardi straightened up and turned to me with dignity. "I'll be back in two weeks." He handed Chloe to me and then turned quickly and walked away with the air of confidence the world stage expected from him.

CHLOE WAS MESMERIZED as Judge Judy made her final rul-
ing of the day. "You ought to be ashamed of yourself," the
judge said with mock vehemence. She lowered her gavel and
growled, "Now get out of my courtroom."

After the show credits flew past, the same reporter from
earlier reappeared on screen with his microphone in hand.
My stomach turned over.

"They travel mall to mall advertising these maintenance-
free pets perfect for kids six and up," he said. A young girl in
ponytails standing beside the reporter gushed, "They seem so
cuddly and cute. I have to have one!"

Behind them, sugar gliders jumped and soared through the
air as a crowd of mall onlookers tittered with enthusiasm. The
reporter continued, "But animal experts familiar with sugar
gliders say this company may be misleading consumers on
the care required to keep these exotic pets alive and healthy.
Some animal right activists suggest even that they are bred in
inhumane conditions and that they are undernourished and
treated poorly."

I winced. "Inhumane?" I reserve that term for instances of
animal cruelty: starvation, abandonment, and neglect. Though
local animal rights activists bring attention to many injustices
done to animals and their work can be instrumental in saving
animals' lives, I had seen no indication that Simon was inten-
tionally causing harm to his gliders. I threw up my arms. "Since
when did animal rights get involved in this?"

"And now," the reporter continued, "a local veterinarian
reports a rash of sick, malnourished, and dying gliders coming into local offices, all sold from mall kiosks."

My jaw dropped to the floor. Marnie looked similarly
stunned.

"Laurie?" she said with ambiguity.

"Not me," I shot back.

A local veterinarian, the reporter said. Who are they talking about? Who would that be? I wracked my mind. Wait a minute, I thought. No, it couldn't have been . . . Hannah? Had she gone to the press with this? I'd called upon her to advise and help me. All this media attention was not going to help. I was running my hands through my hair again, trying to make sense of it all, when my phone vibrated from inside my lab coat pocket. I jerked it out.

It was Simon. I reluctantly pressed answer.

"Why did you go to a reporter with this?" His voice was shaking. I could hear the anger and the hurt. "I thought we were trying to work this out . . . together."

"Simon," I appealed, "it wasn't me. I'm surprised as you are. I think a colleague of mine in Long Island may have talked to this reporter."

"Well, it's all over for me now. Winslow Mall is pulling the kiosk. As soon as the story ran, they started getting irate phone calls and emails. There's even an online petition circulating now to block any mall from selling sugar gliders. A mall representative said to me, 'The mall strives to offer programs that add value to shoppers' experience.' In other words, they don't want the bad press. Neither does my distributor. They're blaming *me*. They're cutting me as a supplier and returning the full shipment of gliders back to the farm."

"I'm so sorry, Simon."

"And you won't believe this," he said with sharpness I hadn't heard before. "I was there, at the mall, when the reporter showed up. I'd driven down to Long Island to check out the kiosk like we talked about. I'd just completed a head-to-toe on the operation."

"And . . . what did you find?"

"Nothing!" he nearly shouted. "There's nothing 'inhumane' going on there. The cages are clean. The animals aren't over-crowded. They're not underweight or malnourished; they all have fresh food and water. They're as healthy as when I loaded them onto the trucks."

He lowered his voice. "This rash of sickness—it's coming from somewhere else. You need to tell your colleague that. You need to tell anyone who asks you that our company was founded on the idea of making sure these animals are adopted out in an ethically responsible way."

"Why don't you make a public statement?" I suggested delicately.

"I'm not talking to the press." Simon shot back. "They've already decided I'm guilty."

He hung up, and my legs wobbled. I reached out for the wall, and Marnie stepped in to steady me.

"You okay? When was the last time you checked your blood sugar? Have you eaten today?"

"It's fine, I'm fine," I said. "I never forget that anymore."

Not since I'd helped Betty Frank off the floor a few years before.

BETTY ENTERED THE examination room wearing her infant pet wallaby, Willie, in a BabyBjörn–like carrier on her chest. His eyes were closed, indicating that he was asleep. I smiled at his big, floppy legs sticking out of the carrier, and Betty sank down in the examination room chair and sighed, expressing a note of physical exhaustion common to new mothers.

Wallabies are marsupials, in the same family as sugar gliders and kangaroos. Female wallabies have a pouch in which their babies nurse and grow. To help the animals adjust to living among people, I encourage wallaby owners to carry their pets in a similar front pack for several weeks, if not longer, until they are socialized.

"Do we really have to do this?" she asked.

"It's a common procedure, and I promise he won't feel anything. General anesthesia and a few hours to rest and recover."

We try to neuter wallabies like Willie when they're young. Once they are full-grown adults, they're much harder to handle. The largest species of wallaby can grow up to six feet tall. I'd not treated a wallaby of this size, but even the smaller ones have strong back legs that enable them to jump and a broad, long tail that they use for balance and support. Over the years, I'd been kicked around by a few.

Betty asked, "Do you have any candy in here? I'm feeling a little woozy."

"I have some gum, but it's sugar free," I said as I turned around to grab a stick off the back examination table.

"Your wallaby looks a little heavy," I said while searching around for my pack of Orbit Wintermint. "Be sure you're feeding him the less sugary stuff, too."

Wallabies are prone to developing a condition called "lumpy jaw," a bacterial infection in the jaw to which sugary treats in an imbalanced diet can contribute.

"Ah, here it is," I said, retrieving the pack from behind a box of Kleenex. I turned around to hand Betty a stick, and she was sliding off her chair. The chair had wheels, and they were rolling out from under her and in my direction. I instinctively moved forward to catch her, but not in time. *Bang!* She fell to the floor and knocked her head. Willie, stuffed tightly into his front pack, felt and heard the thud of Betty hitting the floor and opened his eyes wide. His ears perked straight up, and he began to struggle to wriggle free, clearly aware that his "mama" was in distress. I panicked. What should I do? She appeared to be suffering from critically low blood sugar, a diabetic condition I was very familiar with myself. I quickly grabbed a syringe full of 50 percent dextrose—sugar water, effectively, the kind we administer to hypoglycemic and diabetic animals—but just as I was about to stick her, I stopped myself. *I can't inject Betty. She's not an animal; she's a person. I'm not that kind of doctor.* I'd treated diabetes in ferrets, guinea pigs, and birds before and had even published papers about the endocrine disorder in the *Journal of the American Veterinary Medical Association.* I'd written about how diagnosing and treating diabetes in exotic animals was nearly impossible, as most exotics require minute—almost immeasurable—amounts of insulin to manage the disease, and it's often hard to know exactly what dosage, based on their regular diet, they need. I looked down at Betty as I held the shot of dextrose in my hand, and though tempted to give it to her, I couldn't pretend that I was a physician, legally licensed to treat people. So instead I did what I knew I could safely do: I filled a glass of water from the sink and got down on the floor next to her. I propped her head on my leg and stroked Willie to calm him.

"Betty, can you hear me?"

When she opened her mouth to speak, I said, "Drink this down."

"Thank you," she said and lifted it to her lips, still shaky and unsteady. "I'm a diabetic," she slurred. "This is what happens when you forget to eat." Betty reached down and tugged at Willie's fuzzy ears.

"Mama's okay, now," she whispered. As she continued to massage his ears, his body seemed to relax, and he sank back down into his pouch carrier. After about five more minutes sitting on the floor, I helped Betty back up into her chair. When she assured me she was feeling better, I ran down the hall and fetched her a string cheese and an apple from my own stash in the kitchen.

I'd sworn in that moment that I'd never put myself in a similar position, and mostly I'd kept to that promise.

MARNIE GAVE ME an admonishing look and wagged her finger. "Don't let me catch you lying to me." She turned to Elliot. "Go get Laurie a string cheese out of the fridge, would you?" Marnie led me gently by the arm down the hall to my office.

"Sit down and take five. Eat your cheese, and *then* call Hannah. You need your strength before the next confrontation." She squeezed my shoulder and left me alone.

I sat and ate my cheese, and then I dialed Hannah's number, anticipating that the call would be forwarded again to voice mail. This time, she answered on the first ring.

"Laurie, I assume you're calling about the TV coverage," she started right in. "And I should have warned you, but I really hoped he wouldn't take it this far."

"He? Who? It wasn't you who called this reporter?"

"No," Hannah firmly defended. "Did you think I'd called? I'm sure it was Dr. Barnes. He's a cat and dog vet down the road. A real pill, between you and me. Makes everything his business."

"I'm confused. I thought you made the call. How did this other doctor get involved in this?"

"He read about the recent glider deaths on the message board on Vets Connect. You do know all of your postings are public, don't you?"

"Uh, sure," I shrugged. I hadn't thought to make the postings private; I'd hoped that by casting a wide net within the community, I'd have a better chance of receiving help or at least a lead as to where the illness was coming from.

"Dr. Barnes read your posts, so he knew that gliders were sick and dying in Bedford Hills, and then when he learned that sugar gliders were on sale at Winslow Mall, he called me. Asked me if I knew anything about it, if I'd treated any sick gliders on Long Island."

"And what did you tell him?"

"That I had not admitted any sick gliders to my hospital but that you and I were aware of recent events in the area and that we were working closely together to determine the source of illness and prevent any spread."

"Anything else? How did he link Sugar Buddies specifically to the glider deaths?"

Hannah cleared her throat. "Laurie, I had no idea he'd go to a local reporter with this."

I squeezed my eyes shut. *She'd told him everything.*

"I'm so sorry," she said.

I took a deep breath. There was no sense getting mad at Hannah. It had been only a matter of time before people started putting two and two together, just as I had.

"It's okay," I said. "Still, I can't believe he'd go to a reporter with this. His accusations that the animals are malnourished and treated poorly just aren't true. Unless you discovered something in the blood test results and films? Did you?"

"No, nothing you hadn't already identified. I explained to him that none of the sick gliders you treated had any signs of abuse or neglect, but he wouldn't listen to me. He was on his soapbox, insisting, 'This is what happens when you breed these animals at mills and schlep them from place to place like circus animals. They get sick.'" Hannah paused. "I don't agree with how he handled it, but the adoption operation does sound a little impersonal. Don't you think?"

"It's untraditional, sure. But I don't think we can call it inhumane."

"But—" she said cautiously.

"But what?"

"We just can't ignore that these animals are dying."

"Ignore?" I shot back defensively. That sugar gliders were getting sick was *all* I could think about. Helpless animals were dying under my care nearly every day despite all my efforts to save them. I despaired at the image of Mathilda deteriorating at the bottom of her cage now.

"I'm sorry," Hannah retracted. "I shouldn't have said it that way. I just meant that maybe we should consider whether some of what Dr. Barnes is saying might be true."

I felt that I was on the verge of tears again, but I willed them back. With measured calm, I said, "Until we determine the source of illness, we can't point fingers. We need more information. Dr. Barnes doesn't have the whole story. None of us do. But there are a number of vets across the country, including you and me, committed to figuring this out. If Dr. Barnes calls you again, kindly ask him to stop speaking to the press. Or I will."

"I'll do it," she conceded. "But Laurie, between you and me, aren't you just a little bit suspicious of this company?"

"I don't know, Hannah. I just don't know yet."

4:30 P.M.

I CONTINUED TO play my conversation with Hannah over and over again in my head. Was Sugar Buddies in some way responsible for the dozens of sugar glider deaths across the country—what some of my colleagues were now calling an "epidemic"? What was I missing? Caught up in my back-and-forth thoughts, when I stepped out of my office and into the hallway, I didn't notice Alan, our delivery guy, with a bag of bird food in one arm and Alan the degu in the other. I ran right into them. When we collided, the rodent dropped to the floor and went scurrying down the hall with its tail between his legs.

"Degu down!" I cried and went running in his direction. I chased Alan down the hall until I caught up with him. I reached down and snatched him. When I straightened up, I stopped abruptly. Maxine, Georgie's owner, was standing in the middle of the waiting room.

"Doctor Hess," her voice was shaking. "I'm sorry I didn't return your call the other day, but I just didn't want to talk any more about Georgie's passing. But then I just saw the TV report about the company that sells sugar gliders from malls." She began to tear up, and her cheeks flushed red. "I bought Georgie from a Sugar Buddies mall kiosk in Connecticut. Is that why he got so sick?"

With my dark curls obscuring my face and an agitated degu struggling under my arm, I stepped forward and embraced

Maxine. I wasn't sure what to tell her, other than that, again, Georgie's death was not her fault.

 **6:30 P.M.**

I THANKED MAXINE for making what must have been, for her, a very difficult trip to the hospital and assured her that my colleagues and I were working as hard as we could to determine the cause of Georgie's death, when I remembered my plans to meet Peter at the Gathering Hole, our favorite spot in downtown Mount Kisco. As we had been rushing out the door this morning, going in our separate directions, I'd suggested we meet there for happy hour, just the two of us, for a quick glass of wine in a cozy booth, before I returned to the hospital for another late night of monitoring Lily and Mathilda.

"My treat"—I wrapped my arms around him before he got into his car—"for picking Luke up from school yesterday. And for being the most accommodating husband ever."

"I won't argue with that," he said with a wink.

But now I was late. I hoped that Peter would be in a generous mood. I hurried out the door, crunching along the snowy path to the parking lot. After the initial roar of the ignition, I couldn't help but notice how quiet it was in the car. No squawks, screeches, howls, or screams. In many ways, the sudden absence of noise was louder than anything I'd heard all day. I drove quietly along Route 117 to the Gathering Hole, allowing the silence to envelope me until I heard a familiar voice—my own—and it was clearly saying, "Laurie, slow down." I backed off the accelerator and resumed the speed limit, arriving at our favorite downtown pub nearly thirty minutes late.

It took my eyes a moment to adjust to the dark interior, and I scanned the low-lit bar. I didn't spot Peter there. I peeked into the dining room, and he wasn't there either. As I pulled out my phone to text him, the receptionist approached me. "It's Laurie, isn't it?"

"Yes, I'm looking for Peter, my husband."

She smiled. "He said you'd probably still be wearing your lab coat."

"Oh, jeez," I said as I looked down. "I'm always doing this. Did he call?" I wondered if Peter was running late too. That would be a first.

"No," she said apologetically. "He was here and then he left. Said he'd meet you at home."

I'd done it again—I was too late.

I FOUND PETER sitting quietly on the couch in the family room, wearing the same discontented expression he reserves for Brett and Luke when they push him too far. I immediately registered his disappointment on a grand scale. I approached him slowly.

"I'm so sorry . . . " I started to say.

Peter shook his head, held up his hand in protest, and said, "Stop."

So I did. I stopped short, in the middle of the living room, and continued to stand there until Peter motioned for me to sit down. I sat on the opposite side of the couch facing him and quietly waited. I thought back to a pre-boxing-match celebrity party that Peter's company had sponsored a few years before. He had been so excited to take me along because rumor had it that Annabella Sciorra from *The Sopranos* would be making an appearance. Peter has always asserted that I resemble her, so we thought it'd be fun to do a side-by-side comparison. But before we had the opportunity, I received an emergency call from the hospital.

"I have to take this call," I had said apologetically to Peter.

"You're going to miss Annabella," he said with a frown. "Can't it wait?"

I'd promised to return quickly, but the only place I could get a clear signal was outside the arena, on the street. Teetering up and down the sidewalk in my satin high heels and a red strapless gown, I tried to reassure the owner of a mynah bird whose blood vessel he'd nicked during a routine wing-feather trimming. He couldn't get the bleeding to stop, and he was panicked. I explained how to apply pressure and cornstarch to the bleeding feather to get it to clot. By the time I returned to the cocktail party, nearly an hour had passed. I walked up and looped my arm through Peter's, hoping he'd forgive my delay. He leaned into me and said in a curt whisper, "You're too late."

He said the same words again now, and there was no arguing with him.

"Laurie, we made a deal a long time ago that I wouldn't nag you about your health or your long hours at the hospital, or even your pet family, so long as you also take care of this one—me and the boys. It's about balance, about meeting in the middle, and tonight you didn't meet me anywhere. You left me sitting at a table alone."

He stood up and walked toward the stairs. I could hear Luke in his room playing his upcoming recital piece on his piano keyboard. Peter turned back toward me and said wearily, "I know you have to return to the hospital."

"Just for a few hours," I said, then added as a consolation, "but I can stay here for a while before I go back."

"The boys are already fed, and their homework's nearly done. I told them you'd be coming home late, so why don't you just go ahead. No sense telling them you're home when you just have to leave again."

The piano notes of John Mayer's "Dreaming with a Broken Heart" pierced me. In that moment all I wanted to do was climb the stairs and stand quietly behind Luke as he played so tenderly. I dropped my eyes to the floor. What Peter was saying was regrettably true. When the boys learned that I wasn't staying to say good night and tuck them in, they'd be more disappointed than if they hadn't seen me at all. I stayed planted on the couch in the family room until I heard Peter close our upstairs bedroom door. He was right; I'd lost the balance. School plays, soccer games, Peter's business dinners—I had missed so many events since I opened the hospital that I had stopped counting. The years were rolling by, and if I didn't start making more time for Peter and the boys, I would lose moments I could never get back. I stood up and only then noticed Dale on his perch in the corner of the room. He was so quiet, not his usual squawky self. He must be feeling the tension too. I tearfully slipped outside the door and drove the dark streets back toward the hospital.

5

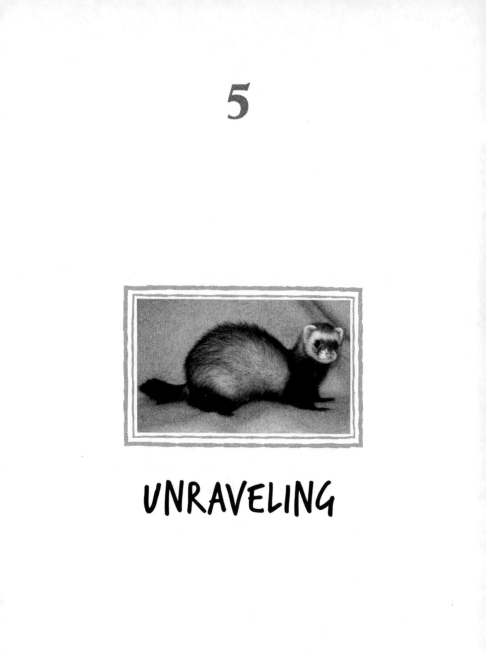

UNRAVELING

FRIDAY, 8:20 A.M., BEDFORD ROAD

I was shivering in the car and willing the engine to hurry up with the heat. I took a long gulp of coffee and a bite of my egg-white sandwich before steering onto Bedford Road. I drove wearily toward the hospital, recalling Peter's and my conversation from the night before. It was well after two in the morning when I'd finally slid into bed next to him. He didn't say anything, but I knew he was awake. Peter truly embraces the popular mantra of many married couples: don't go to bed angry. He simply cannot rest until he feels some sense of resolve. So with his back to me, I began to tell him the story of Carl and Molly and their beloved ferret, Bandit.

Molly and Carl did not have human children, but over the years they'd created a family of ferrets. Bandit, with his dark brown mask and a sable-colored, slender body, was now their only remaining child, and they doted on him endlessly, sparing no expense on his care. They traveled regularly to my clinic from their home in Manhattan, where ferrets are not legal (yet half-naked men dressed up as cowboys singing in

Times Square are), for general checkups, dental cleanings, and nail trimmings. Typically Carl brought Bandit into the hospital, and they were always welcome visitors in the constant chaos of my day. He'd greet me with a big fatherly hug and a warm "How's it going, kiddo?"

Probably in his early seventies, Carl was twice as energetic as I. He ran marathons, swam laps daily, and traveled extensively. I envied his stamina and also his impeccable style. I couldn't remember a hospital visit when Carl had not appeared in a neat shirt and freshly polished shoes. He had once shared with me the story of buying Molly an engagement ring nearly a dozen years after they were married. He'd found the ring in a roadside antique shop he'd stumbled upon while driving along the North Shore of Massachusetts. The diamond ring was in a box of tarnished and "junky-looking" jewelry, he'd said. He'd bought it on a whim and was surprised to discover, once he'd had it cleaned and appraised by a dealer in New York City's diamond district, that the stone was nearly flawless and worth a great deal. Carl finally proposed "properly" to Molly at a French bistro in Chelsea.

It had been nearly a year since I'd seen either Carl or Molly. I knew that they'd moved from Manhattan to South Jersey, and I'd often wondered how they were doing, so I was happy when I saw that Bandit was scheduled for a routine checkup.

I was already in the examination room when Marnie led Molly and Bandit in and closed the door. I was surprised to see Molly without Carl and concerned that she looked especially worn. She held Bandit in the crook of her arm, and he looked around curiously. I wondered why she'd made the three-hour drive from southern New Jersey on icy roads instead of Carl.

"It's so nice to see you." I reached out and lightly squeezed her arm and stroked Bandit's dark fur. "It's usually your husband who brings in Bandit. Where is Carl today?"

Molly sat down with Bandit and burst into tears.

"Molly?"

"He's gone," she whispered.

"Gone?" I was confused. Gone where? I wasn't certain what she meant.

"Carl had a massive heart attack."

"Oh, my God!" I gasped. "When?"

"Six months ago." She choked and put Bandit down on the ground. The playful animal darted under the examination table and began sniffing around, looking for a tight space to squeeze his lanky body into, as ferrets love to do. "I'm so sorry. I was going to call you, but I just couldn't do it."

I knelt down in front of Molly. I took particular notice of the engagement ring that Carl had been so proud of. It really was stunning, an emerald-cut solitaire set in yellow gold. "I understand. You don't have to apologize."

"There are just so many memories here of Carl, you know?" Her lips turned up in a sad smile as she watched Bandit attempt to climb up the slippery metal legs of the examination table. He'd make it about halfway up before he slid down again. "He loved this little rascal so much," she mused. "Bandit was always stealing Carl's shoes and hiding them around the house. Carl would just laugh it off and chase him up and down the stairs, through the living room, and out the back door." Molly paused as she held back more tears. "I'd scold him for playing too rough. 'You're going to break your neck,' I'd say, and he'd just wave me off and he and Bandit would carry on. Said Bandit kept him young."

"Or the other way around," I said, smiling. "Carl was such a vibrant man."

Molly swallowed hard. "He was."

I thought of Peter, of how much he meant to me and how devastating it must be to lose your lifelong partner.

"We never had children," she said after several moments. "We had each other. That was enough for us. And then, of course"—she smiled—"we had our ferrets."

"Just as much work as children," I smiled back.

"Carl wouldn't have had it any other way. Bandit's our last ferret, and he was Carl's best pal."

I picked up Bandit as he scurried by and handed him back to Molly.

"Come here, you," she said and rubbed her thumb against Bandit's head. The loving ferret leaned his head into the caress, and I could see that Bandit was equally bonded with Molly. Her grief was etched around her eyes. "I can hardly get through the days without my husband, Dr. Hess. But at least I still have Bandit. Carl didn't leave me alone."

WHEN I FINISHED my story, I reached out and placed my hand on Peter's back. I could only just see the outline of my wedding rings in the darkness.

"I will never again leave you sitting at a table alone," I whispered. "I'm so sorry that I did."

Peter inhaled and slowly rolled over. "Laurie," he sighed.

"You were absolutely right to get mad at me," I blurted out. "I know I've been doing a horrible job at balancing everything, you and the boys especially. I'm not going to make any excuses."

Peter turned on his side and faced me. "I don't want to be upset with you." His eyes softened. "I just want a night out with my wife, okay?"

I smiled with teary relief and nodded. "Okay."

"Do you happen to know when she might be available?"

"I'll check her schedule first thing in the morning." I leaned over and hugged him. Dale who'd been silent in his sleeping cage, suddenly stirred and burst out, "IT'S A PARTY, IT'S A PARTY."

You can teach parrots to say just about anything, and if you're not careful, they will often learn things you don't want them to. Dale's declaring "It's a party" was an improvement from past comments. When Brett was a colicky baby, I'd spend hours late at night and early in the morning trying to nurse him to sleep. It always seemed that once I'd finally gotten him to settle down and put him in his crib, Dale would burst out screeching. Peter would jump up out of bed and shout back at him, "Shut up, dummy!"

I tried to explain to Peter that yelling at Dale would only encourage him to screech more. Yelling at a bird for making undesirable noise simply reinforces the behavior by reward-ing him with attention each time he does so, which is what happened in our house: Dale would screech, Peter would yell, and Dale would screech louder. And then, Dale began to yell back at Peter, "Shut up, dummy." The heated exchanges went on until we changed our strategy and began to ignore Dale when he made noise and reward him when he was quiet. When he wasn't screeching and waking up the baby, we'd give him treats, verbal praise, a head pat, or a favorite toy. It took a few months, but as we continued to praise Dale for keeping his beak shut, he yelled less, and finally everyone was able to get some sleep.

I TOOK ANOTHER sip of coffee and turned down the car heater. I can do this, I thought. I can balance my career, my health, my kids, and my marriage. It's all about knowing how to manage everyone's needs—who needs what when and how to give it to them. I counsel pet owners on how to do this every day. It's a delicate, ever-changing balance but an essential one if you are going to have pets. I recollected one such instance that had begun with a frantic early-morning phone call from Miriam Betts.

"Doctor," she said with urgency, "I think he's exploded!"

"Slow down," I said. "Who's exploded?"

"Harry, my husband's rat."

"Is your husband available to bring him in?"

"He's out of the country on business," she said with contempt, indicating that her husband was the bigger rat.

"Hmmm," I said. A rat—exploded? That would be a first for me, although the veterinarian practice is full of surprises. "Can you tell me exactly what you see?"

"I walked in just now to change his food and water, and there's this mess everywhere."

"And you're not sure what it is?"

"It's disgusting," Miriam said as if she were standing in it now. "Pink and slimy."

"Okay, here's what I want you to do. Put on a pair of dishwashing gloves and pack the cage into the car. Meet me at the hospital. Can you do that?" I asked.

Twenty minutes later, Miriam dropped the cage onto the examination table and shuddered, "Yuck."

One look into Harry's cage, and the "explosion" started to make some sense. First of all, Harry wasn't actually a rat but an exceptionally hefty house mouse. A cute one, too, I thought, with a snowy white belly and a cinnamon-speckled face. Also, Harry had just given birth to a healthy litter of baby mice.

Twenty-two, to be exact.

I smiled. "Congratulations are in order. Harry didn't explode; he just had babies."

Miriam furrowed her brow and tentatively leaned into the cage. "Those are babies?"

Relaxing in a bed of sawdust with her eyes closed, the house mouse looked quite cozy and content with her litter of peanut-sized pups affectionately nuzzling her.

"Yes, and maybe you should consider changing Harry's name to Harriet."

Miriam didn't seem to find my suggestion amusing or helpful. She looked back into the cage with the same severe expression she'd worn since she had arrived. She studied the heap of newborns.

I opened the cage and carefully rolled one into my hand. "We call them 'pinkies' because they're hairless and pink at birth. And they're actually not slimy, just a little wet from coming out of Mama's belly."

Miriam grimaced. "Where are their ears?"

"Baby mice are born blind and deaf, which is why their ears are stuck to the sides of their heads. It doesn't look like they have any, but see," I said pointing to a thin, pink fold of skin on the side of the newborn's head. "That's an ear. Their eyes kind of look like they're sealed shut too."

"Well, those don't look like mice to me," Miriam said and backed away.

"They do look kind of alien, I agree, but that will all change in a couple of days. They'll begin to grow hair, and within a month they'll look like little versions of their mama." I smiled. "It's really quite fascinating to watch."

"Fascinating?" Miriam turned sharply toward me. "My husband's out of the country, Dr. Hess. I cannot take care of twenty-two babies."

"I understand it may seem like a lot," I reassured her, "but you really won't have to do much."

"No!" She raised her voice. "You're not hearing me—twenty-two babies are *too much!*"

Miriam was shouting at me, so I definitely heard her. I could empathize, too: for her, twenty-two baby mice were twenty-two more than she could bear. I got it; we all have our tipping point. Still, I wasn't about to take in her new family of mice.

"Okay," I said. "Let's figure this out. When will your husband be home?"

"Not for another six days," she said, nostrils flaring.

"These first days are important," I said calmly, "but they're manageable. As long as Harriet does her job attending to and feeding her babies, you really won't have to intervene."

"And what if she doesn't do her job?"

"Then call me." I decided not to share with Miriam that if Harriet did ignore her twenty-two babies, they would need to be fed commercially available formula for baby rodents through a dropper every two hours and provided with a small warm box heated to about eighty degrees Fahrenheit; they would also need to have their bellies gently rubbed with a

Q-tip after feeding to stimulate digestion. I knew that detailed list of instructions would likely send Miriam over the edge, so I said, "Let's assume for now that everything will go fine. And then after your husband returns home we can help you find new homes for all of these baby mice."

"He'll be looking for a new home too," Miriam muttered.

"You can do this," I said. "Take a deep breath. It will be okay." And I inhaled deeply myself. Miriam grudgingly followed my lead.

9:20 A.M., ANIMAL HOSPITAL

I ARRIVED IN the hospital parking lot and glanced around for Bob's truck. I didn't see it as I usually did. I thought back to Jeanne's visit yesterday. "We cannot afford to keep these animals alive," she'd said. I wondered if Bob's absence this morning had anything to do with her icy threat.

I opened the hospital doors to what sounded like a bird sanctuary. A screech owl was letting out deafening shrieks, and Target was chanting, "CHICKEN, CHICKEN, I'M A CHICKEN."

"CHICKEN, CHICKEN, I'M A CHICKEN," imitated Stop.

Target and Stop had been playing this repetitive game ad nauseam ever since I had treated Mr. Larsen's hens for reproductive problems more than a month ago. I was half expecting them to begin clucking any day now.

Colette took a deep, measured breath, stood up from behind the reception desk, and glared at Target and Stop. Standing nearly six feet tall, she could loom over the desk like an elementary school teacher and command silence with just a look.

Not unexpectedly, a hush fell over the waiting room as Target and Stop took her cue and quieted in their cage.

"Good morning," I whispered as I approached her desk. "Has Bob called?"

"No," she whispered back, "but Hannah just did. She's just admitted a sick glider to her clinic."

"Oh, no. Not another one."

"And," Colette continued, "a group from Long Island's local animal rights chapter picketed her hospital this morning."

"Okay, this is getting out of control."

As I was processing both pieces of bad news, Marnie appeared with another. She put her hands on her hips and gave me an admonishing look. "You were very busy last night, weren't you?"

"What do you mean?"

"Only that the Vets Connect message board this morning is having a field day with you, and outraged pet owners on sites like GliderGab are posting things like 'Local Vet Denies Inhumane Practices.'"

I groaned. "Why do they keep using that word?" I rubbed my eyes.

"You look terrible," Marnie said. "Are you getting sick?"

"I'm just tired," I mumbled and thought back to my late-night activities online. I had been busy. After coming home from the hospital and peeking in on Brett and Luke, both stretched out sideways with their feet dangling off their beds, I'd retreated to my home office to make my own countercharge to Dr. Barnes's claim that Sugar Buddies was mistreating its animals and that its operation was circus-like and inhumane. I felt compelled to refute Dr. Barnes and also to stand up, once again, for Simon, who I still believed had the animals' health and safety in mind. What had Simon said to me? "Our company was founded on the idea of making sure these animals are adopted out in an ethically responsible way." But Simon had been firm that he wasn't going to speak to the press, so given my natural ability to run my mouth, I did.

I created several versions of the following statement and posted it on Vets Connect, on my hospital's Facebook page, and on a few public message boards for owners of exotic pets:

I appreciate people's concerns that Sugar Buddies' adoption procedures are certainly different from more traditional methods and that adopting pets out of mall kiosks seems like an impersonal way to find these animals homes, but to call their practices inhumane, I think, is an exaggeration.

I've spoken at length with Sugar Buddies' chief breeder, and my understanding is that their operation is in fact humane—their shipping practices are clean and safe, and once the animals are in the malls, the company can retain tight control over their care until they're adopted. In fact, by selling directly through their mall kiosks, the company can effectively find loving families for hundreds of animals that need new homes.

Of course I'm concerned that sugar gliders are becoming sick and dying, but I haven't been able to attribute how Sugar Buddies are raising, treating, or selling their animals to the unfortunate deaths. My staff and I are doing everything we can at the animal hospital to treat every sick glider that comes through our doors, and we will continue to work with other veterinarians to help determine the source of the illness.

I looked back at Marnie who was now tilting her head with concern. "Laurie, are you sure you want to continue to defend these guys?"

"Until I have a solid reason not to."

"Hannah just admitted another one of their gliders. How much more reason do you need?"

I wearily slogged back toward my office wondering if maybe Marnie was right. Maybe I should ease up on my public discourse and my defense of Simon. Perhaps I'd spoken too fervently on his behalf. I'd now publicly aligned myself with a company that had more than a few questions to answer. Meanwhile, Lily and Mathilda weren't getting any better, and more gliders were becoming sick.

I found Elliot in my office, huddled over the keyboard, scrolling through my inbox, which I'd asked him to do. "Flag anything that may be a lead."

He startled when he heard me and swiveled around in his chair.

"Morning," he said while making an awkward attempt to block the computer screen.

"Let me guess—I've offended a few more people?"

Elliot scratched his head. "Um," he stalled.

"Wow, that many? What do they have to say?"

"Doctor, some of these comments are kind of"—he continued to waver—"harsh. And there have been phone calls too."

"Go ahead. I can take it."

"Okay, but don't say I didn't warn you." He turned around in his chair, and I took a seat beside him. "This one is from a shopper petitioning Sugar Buddies to stop selling sugar gliders throughout the region. She says, "These animals require more time to care for than the company lets on, and that's why they're getting sick."

I addressed the computer screen as if I were responding to the writer in person. "Like most any animal, without proper care and nutrition or attention to their special needs, sugar gliders are at risk of getting sick. And"—I held up a finger to emphasize my next point—"understanding an animal's needs is ultimately the responsibility of the owner. What's next?" I said to Elliot.

"This woman says sugar gliders aren't meant to be domesticated and live in captivity. She says sugar gliders can't thrive behind bars."

"Well she's certainly entitled to her opinion, but I disagree that domesticating gliders is a criminal act. If it were, I guess that makes me an accomplice."

Elliot raised a skeptical eyebrow. "Do you want me to keep reading them?"

I nodded. "Sorry, I'm tired and testy. Yes, go on."

Elliot continued to recite objection after objection: "How can you defend that shady company?" "These animals shouldn't be confined in small cages." "Defending Sugar Buddies is unethical." "How can you align yourself with a company that is killing innocent animals?"

I finally put a hand of resignation up in the air. "Okay, enough." I cut Elliot off in mid-sentence. "I get it. I'm not winning any popularity contests this morning." I understood that people were feeling angry, frustrated, and desperate. I was too. And I appreciated that many of these comments were coming from people who had sick animals or were grieving pets they'd recently lost. Given the range of emotions associated with this case and with no clear understanding of what was making so many baby gliders ill, I could understand how the public and some of my veterinary colleagues were questioning and even outwardly critical of my defense of Sugar Buddies. And yet, I'd only meant to raise an objective voice. Unfortunately, my intent had been lost in translation, and now my words were coming back to bite me. I sat back in my chair, regretting the position I'd put myself in.

"Also, a Dr. Barnes has been direct-messaging you all morning."

"He has?" I leaned forward and squinted at the blinking square box in the corner of the screen. "I'm not wearing my readers. What does it say?"

Elliot reluctantly read the message: "Dr. Hess, your insensitivity in this matter shocks me. Animals are sick and dying. Whose side are you on?"

I was already feeling beat up, and now I felt as though I'd been slapped in the face. I stared at the screen in shock, feeling the sting of his words.

"Dr. Hess?" Elliot said.

It took me a minute to recover, and when I did, I was enraged. Before I could catch myself, I screamed back at the screen, "On the side of the animals, you jerk!"

Elliot flinched.

I stood up abruptly. "If anyone else calls or messages or texts to tell me I'm an insensitive doctor and an all-around horrible person," I sputtered, "you can tell them that I'm in the isolation ward doing everything in my power to save the life of another dying glider. And if that's not enough, well then send me to jail!"

I stormed out of the office before I could message Dr. Barnes back with more words I'd later regret.

Marnie was already in the isolation ward checking on Mathilda, who was lying facedown on the cage floor with her tiny limbs tucked tightly underneath her. Marnie had to prod her just to be sure she was still alive. Her breathing was labored and shallow, indicating that she was in extreme pain. Marnie gave me a look that I understood implicitly. My anger dissolved, right then and there, into anguish. I stood with Mathilda for several minutes stroking her fur, accepting the reality of her condition. I couldn't save her. I took a deep breath and faced the job I had before me.

"I'll make the call," I said and turned back toward the door. And yet, when I opened it, there was Bob, leaning up against the wall and looking even more exhausted than he had the day before.

"You're here," I said, surprised. "I was just about to call you."

He opened his mouth but couldn't seem to form any words.

"Come with me in the back." I gently guided him down the hall into the break room. "Can I get you something to drink?"

"Coffee would be good. Just black."

I poured myself a cup too and sat directly across from him. "I was just about to call you to talk about Mathilda's condition."

"Can I speak first?"

I nodded and set my cup on the table.

He paused for a moment. "I made a decision last night. As much as I don't want to give up on her, I can see that she's in pain." He looked down at the table. "Unless you're about to tell me that something has changed . . . " Bob raised his eyes to meet mine.

"Nothing has changed." I shook my head sadly.

"Well then"—he cleared his throat as he choked on the words—"I think it's time."

"Do you mean . . . to euthanize her?" I asked quietly.

He nodded.

I reached out and put my hand on his. The rough calluses on his fingers didn't match the softness of his voice. Of all the things I would have to address today, Bob's grief would no doubt be the heaviest. We sat in silence, both of us letting the reality of his decision sink in. In fact, it was the same conclusion I'd come to, and Bob had just beat me to it.

"Bob, I'm so sorry." Tears welled up in my own eyes. "I've tried everything."

"I know that you have. I don't blame you,"

I don't often feel the need for pet owners' reassurance that they know I've done my best, but in this case I felt huge relief at Bob's words. I wondered if he'd seen my statement online defending Sugar Buddies.

"I've been working closely with the company that you adopted Mathilda from and with other vets across the country, too, to locate the source of illness," I paused. "But I still don't know what is making her so sick." I shook my head regrettably. My first interest in veterinary medicine was internal medicine because I love solving problems—putting an animal's symptoms together to arrive at a single diagnosis so that I can provide treatment. I looked into Bob's sad eyes. "At this point, I don't know what more I can do to save her." I couldn't think back to a time when I'd failed so absolutely to help an animal in need of care.

After a moment of silence, Bob said, "I want to be with her. Right with her until the end."

I left him alone in the break room, and Marnie met me just outside the door.

"He's signing the formal permission form for euthanasia," I said.

10:30 A.M., SURGICAL ROOM

WE'D GIVEN MATHILDA the first shot, a tranquilizer that would relieve her immediate pain and sedate her enough that she wouldn't be fully conscious when we gave her the final injection, an overdose of pentobarbital. This barbiturate, administered directly into the heart, would immediately end her suffering. As I prepared the injection, I reminded myself to breathe. Though the procedure was predictable and routine, and one I was all too familiar with after so many years of practice, this time felt harder than most. Heartbreaking. I reached out and put my gloved hand on Bob's arm. "Are you sure you want to be here for this?"

"Yes."

"Once I administer the injection, you can stay with her as long as you need to."

He nodded again.

"If you feel ready, now is the time for final good-byes," I said as gently as I could.

Bob picked up Mathilda from where she was resting on top of the exam table, held her to his chest, and whispered into her tiny gray ears. He cradled the little animal in his large, calloused hands with a love so much greater than Mathilda's small size. He stroked the top of her head, and after a few moments she appeared to fall asleep. He lay her back on the examination table, turned to me, and nodded his final consent.

The room went silent other than for the quiet sounds of Mathilda's slow breathing. I parted the fur on Mathilda's chest with an alcohol-soaked cotton ball and injected a tiny volume of euthanasia solution into her heart. Within seconds, her little body went limp.

"Good-bye, sweet girl." Bob was outwardly weeping now, and I was choking up myself. More than ten years before, I'd had to put down Bailey, my cherished gray tabby cat. That easy-to-purr, lovable fluff ball had been my constant companion for nearly two decades. Throughout my twenties, as I trudged through vet school and before I adopted Dale or met and married Peter, Bailey had been by my side. He had eventually become sick from a slow-growing, inoperable liver tumor. One night after my shift at the Animal Medical Center in New York City, I came home to find his frail body collapsed in the corner of my bedroom. I rushed him to the Center, understanding that his time had finally come. There was nothing anyone could do to save him. When I entered the waiting room, I was the client, not the doctor. And the animal I held was my pet, my beloved friend. Bailey lay nearly lifeless in my lap in the intensive care unit as I gave my colleague permission to administer the final injection. I cradled him in my arms, watching the euthanasia fluid pass from the syringe into his veins. Bailey's body tensed at first and then became limp and relaxed.

When I first became a vet, I mistakenly thought this aspect of the job would get easier over time. It doesn't. Losing a pet is one of life's great heartbreaks, and saying good-bye hurts every time. My mentor Dr. Miller said, "Every vet struggles with this. But when an animal is suffering with no chance of survival, you must remind yourself that you are helping, even when it feels extraordinarily sad."

I wiped away my own tears with the sleeve of my lab coat and turned to Bob. "When you're ready, I bet Lily would love to see you."

Lily was the one comfort I could provide Bob in this moment. Mathilda was gone. But Bob's constant companion was still alive.

12:00 P.M., WAITING ROOM

MARNIE HAD PREPARED Mathilda's body for burial by wrapping it in our customary black tissue paper and slipping it into a silver cardboard gift box. I slowly approached Bob where he sat in the waiting room and handed him the small parcel, along with a silk jewelry bag containing a clipping of Mathilda's fur. As he took both from my hands, the waiting room fell silent. I glanced over at Mr. Rasmussen, who was bouncing his baby kinkajou on his lap, and Mrs. Ellis, who was nuzzling her angora bunny, Petunia. She put a sympathetic hand up to her heart as she recognized the somber exchange. She'd been handed a similar box before.

Bob stood up. "Thank you," he mouthed. I tried to say, "You're welcome," but the words caught in my throat. I nodded my head instead and watched silently as he turned and walked out the front doors alone. Knowing that his wife, Jeanne, neither appreciated nor had ever even tried to understand his feelings for his gliders, on this somber day I was sorry Bob would grieve the loss of his Mathilda alone.

2:00 P.M., MY OFFICE

EMOTIONALLY SPENT, I wanted to hole up in my office, pull down the shades, and join Bob in his sorrow, but I somehow summoned my strength for Lily. She was still alive. She had a chance. Lily's movements were slow, and her appetite was poor, but she was holding on. I reasoned that her strength was supported by her age. Lily was over five years old, and Mathilda had been just a baby. Just like the other baby gliders who had died, Mathilda had been too vulnerable to fight off the spreading illness.

Wait a minute. Spreading illness? What if the illness wasn't spreading, at least not in the way I'd thought?

I recalled when Bob had first brought Mathilda and Lily into the hospital and I had presumed that the illness must be contagious since both gliders were sick. And when I had discovered that Pockets, Georgie, and Mathilda had all been adopted from the same Johnson Valley Mall kiosk, I had further suspected that the illness was spreading from animal to animal and cage to cage. Of course I wasn't absolutely sure, as you really cannot know whether an illness is contagious until you know what is causing it, but since both of Bob's gliders were suffering, it seemed very likely that the illness had spread from young Mathilda to Lily.

But now I wondered if my assumption were dead wrong. If the illness was contagious, why had only a handful of Simon's gliders from Johnson Valley Mall become sick? So many gliders in one place in such close contact. If the illness was contagious, the entire population of young animals transported and housed together should all be showing similar symptoms. I wondered the same thing now about Winslow Mall in Long Island. So far, there was only one reported case of illness, and Hannah was treating that failing young glider now.

If the illness wasn't contagious, spreading from glider to glider and mall to mall, there had to be another connection linking the sick gliders in different locations. Instead of studying the commonality of conditions within the mall populations, we should be looking at what the small subset of sick gliders shared in common. What was their special relationship?

I searched through the stack of papers on my desk, looking for Elliot's list. I found it quickly, as it was marked up with highlighter pen. I'd struck a bright yellow line through every city where gliders had been reported sick and dying and where Exotic Essentials distributed Simon's animals. Every city on the list had a yellow mark through it. Except—I took a deep breath—I'd jotted down in the margin of the paper several mall locations: Chicago, Detroit, Tulsa, and St. Louis. In those cities Exotic Essentials had set up mall kiosks, but there had been no reports of illness. Not yet, anyway. I logged in to the Vets Connect message board: no new posts indicating an outbreak of illness in any of those cities. I quickly wrote a new post: "Has anyone treated a sick glider in any of the following locations?" I listed the scattering of states and then wondered aloud why some of Simon's gliders were getting sick when others weren't? In at least five cities across the country, they were seemingly immune.

As I pondered this new information, Marnie poked her head around the office door. I waved her in, and she slid down into the chair next to mine. We often retreated to the office like this after difficult procedures. We sighed in unison.

"That was pretty awful, wasn't it?" The image of Bob cradling Mathilda's still body resurfaced in my mind. "How are you holding up?"

She nodded. "I'm okay."

"I'm so glad you were there. I couldn't have handled that sad scene without you."

Marnie's eyes suddenly filled with tears.

"Marn?" I leaned forward, searching her face.

I was thrown off by her swell of emotion. Even on our hardest days, Marnie is reliably tough. She looked away with a pained expression.

"Hey," I reached out. "We're going to solve this. We're not going to lose another glider. I promise."

She wiped her face with the back of her hand and looked squarely at me. "That's not it."

"What is it, then?"

"This is really not the day to tell you this," she said and paused. "But I've been putting it off for a week."

I sat back in my chair. "What is it?" I asked again.

She took a deep breath. "I've been offered a job with the Los Angeles Exotics Veterinary Specialists."

I heard her, but it took a minute before I could really put the meaning of the words together. Once I did, my stomach tightened, and I thought I might throw up. *No, no, no. Don't say this to me. Take it back.*

"Laurie? Say something."

What could I say? I hadn't seen this coming. I was shocked. Even on my most frazzled days, when I feel pulled in a million directions between home, work, and whatever else, I still keep it pretty well together. Well, at least I think I do a commendable job of acting as if I have it all together. But this completely unraveled me. I felt the heat rush to my cheeks. Before I could stop myself, I clenched my fists like a defiant three-year-old and wailed, "You can't do this! It wasn't our plan!"

This was now my second meltdown moment of the day, and it reminded me of Maryanne Odette, who'd reacted simi-larly when I delivered to her unexpected news.

"She's nesting," I said as I took Ginger, a cockatiel, out of her cage. "That's why she's shredding all this paper." I nodded at the mound of newspaper scraps that Ginger was settling into. "And look at this." I pointed to Ginger's swollen abdo-men. "She's getting ready to lay an egg."

"An egg? I didn't plan for an egg," Maryanne said. "Can you give her an injection or something to make it stop?"

"There's nothing to stop. You may not have planned for it, but it's going to happen regardless. She's a young female bird, and it's almost spring. I suggest you take her home and let nature take its course."

But before Maryanne could respond, Ginger's breathing started to race. She extended her wings and made a loud, clucking sound.

"Oh, boy, here it comes," I said.

Ginger strained against me as she pushed out the egg. *Splat!* The unfertilized egg landed on the floor right at Maryanne's feet. As if relieved to be rid of the extra weight, Ginger took a deep breath. Maryanne and I looked at the broken shell and then back up at each other.

"Nothing to plan for now," I said.

Marnie and I had shared a dream to open a veterinary hospital solely dedicated to birds and exotic pets, where the animals and their clients felt special, not like add-ons at a tra-ditional cat and dog hospital. At our hospital, the care, equipment, and technology reflected the unique needs of those very special animals. We'd realized this dream together. I was proud of what we'd created, and I couldn't imagine continuing the work without her. I'd assumed we'd be walking the same hospital hallways until we were older, grayer, and ready to retire. At the thought of her leaving and of facing the challenging cases and overwrought clients without her, I felt a seismic emptiness. I slid down in my chair.

"This wasn't our plan," I said again, more quietly but still in the voice of a hurt child.

"I know," she said with apology in her voice.

"You're going to take it, aren't you?"

She nodded. "Probably."

"Couldn't you choose somewhere a little closer," I asked, "like the Animal Medical Center in the city? That's only a train ride away."

"Laurie, I wasn't looking for a job. I love our work here. They found me, and as much as I don't want to leave you or this hospital, I have to consider it. You know how hard it is for me to be so far away from my sister in California."

Marnie and her sister, Claudia, were tight. They shared the kind of connection and closeness I'd always craved from my only sibling—my brother, Geoffrey. Even though they lived on opposite coasts, Marnie and Claudia managed to see each other four or five times a year. After Marnie's divorce, she and her sister had started vacationing together. "We do it for the kids," Marnie said, a little defensively, but I knew those so-called family vacations were a guise for Marnie and Claudia to travel to exotic resorts and sip cocktails together poolside.

When Claudia had been diagnosed with cancer eighteen months before, however, she'd stopped traveling. Marnie still made trips out to Los Angeles, but she always returned plagued with guilt and regret that she wasn't more available for her sister. I empathized with her feeling of helplessness; I'd watched my own grandfather advance through the debilitating stages of the disease. I understood and appreciated that an opportunity to work at an esteemed exotic hospital in Los Angeles was a blessing for both Marnie and Claudia.

Still, I wasn't ready to be an understanding friend. Not quite yet.

"I do understand what this opportunity means," I said, attempting to regain some maturity. "And I want to support you. But honestly, Marnie, we just put Mathilda down an hour ago." I ran my hands through my tangled mane and willed myself to remain steady. "I've had as much bad news as I can take today. I can't do this now too."

"Sure, okay," she said softly as I stood up. I could feel her eyes on me as I turned and walked out of the room.

5:30 P.M., BEDFORD ROAD

I WAS HALFWAY home when I began to feel nauseous and jittery. I grasped the steering wheel, realizing I hadn't checked my blood sugar in several hours. It was undoubtedly very low, as I'd missed my afternoon snack and had eaten very little with all the activity at the hospital. How utterly neglectful, I scolded myself. *Laurie, you know better than this.* My hands began to tremble. I knew that once it started, the trembling would be hard to keep under control, and continuing to drive would be unsafe. I pulled off the road and fumbled around in my purse, my hands frantically searching for the protein bar I'd dropped in it this morning. I found it, tore back the wrapping, and jammed it into my mouth. I also pulled out the glucose tablets that I reserve for super blood sugar lows. I popped four of them onto my tongue and swallowed hard. I'm always surprised at how sour they taste, like the SweeTarts candies I craved as a treat as a kid and now rely on as an adult to survive. I thought, who am I, really, to lecture anyone on the importance of preventive care when I don't extend it to myself? Peter's words throbbed in my head. *It's all about balance, Laurie.* I wouldn't tell him about this. I couldn't tell him about this. Not so soon after our argument, and makeup, last night. It would only lead us into another fight. After my blood sugar had normalized nearly ten minutes later, I pulled back onto the road.

I arrived home, turned off the ignition, and sat in the parked car. I recounted the many times like this, after especially long and emotionally difficult days at the hospital, when I'd willed myself to pull it together before going into the house. Marnie had once said, "I think we deal with the pain, heartache, and grief at the hospital the best we can, and then we take the rest of it home. On second thought," she continued, "I actually take it in my car with me. Sometimes I cry all the way home. It's like a bad country-and-western song. By the time I'm done, I'm home!"

I got out of the car, walked up our long driveway, and kicked off my boots as soon as I walked through the back door.

"Is that you, Mom?" I heard Luke ask.

I appeared in the doorframe and forced a cheery smile. Peter and Luke looked up at me from the kitchen table.

"You're home early," Peter said, surprised.

I walked over and gave him a kiss. "'Bout time, don't you think?"

"This doesn't count as our date night, you know?"

I returned his playful grin. "Yes, I know that."

"Mom's here now, so she can help me," Luke said to Peter.

"Well, excuse me," Peter said with exaggeration and motioned me over to a chair. "Please, join us."

I sat down between the two of them and tousled Luke's hair. "Your eyes look better today. Hardly pink at all, but keep taking your eye drops, okay, for the full seven days?"

Luke nodded.

"So whatcha working on?" I changed the subject.

"We're bickering over Luke's science project," Peter answered. "I'm trying to give him a lesson on the law of inertia, the simple concept of friction and motion."

Luke rolled his eyes. "Dad's trying to talk like some scientist, and I have to get this done by tomorrow." He sat back in his chair with the same expression Peter gets when he can't figure out the Sunday crossword. I warmed at their resemblance.

"Remind me what project this is?" I asked Luke.

"It's the egg-drop project. I have to build a device out of paper and sticks that will keep the egg from breaking when we drop it off the roof at school tomorrow."

I stared at Luke. "Did you say the egg-drop project?"

"Yeah, Mom, I just told you that."

I started to laugh at the irony. My son had his own egg-drop project, as if to punctuate the unexpected events of my day. Sometimes when you're not planning for it, life goes *splat!* right before your eyes.

"What's so funny?" Luke knit his brow. "You're acting weird."

I put my hand over my mouth and continued to giggle. And then my eyes filled with tears.

"Are you all right?" Peter regarded me curiously too.

I shook my head and started to cry.

Both Peter and Luke watched me fall apart at the kitchen table. I choked, "The egg really did drop today."

Peter put an arm around me, and as the tears streamed down my face, I finally let myself feel the weight of it all—the day's full range of disappointment, rage, fear, and loss.

6

PIECE BY PIECE

SATURDAY, 8:39 A.M., HOME

I'd slept late and awakened with achy bones, as if I'd been hit by a phantom car in the middle of the night. I squinted at the sunlight pouring in through the shutters of our eighteenth-century windows. Streams of light flooded in through the slats, settling in a warm pool on the wide pine floorboards. Bean, our daft tabby, chased the flickering beams of light around the floor as though they were goldfish just beyond his grasp. Where was Peter? Had he already left for work? I must have slept through his alarm, but how? His sports talk radio always jolted me awake if I wasn't already. The testosterone-charged ribbing typically woke up everyone in the house—it often roused sleepyheads Luke and Brett in their bedrooms down the hall, and the banter also tended to rattle Dale, Quinn, Lennon, and Ringo in their cages. Dale would start first: "Good morning!" Then from the next room, Quinn would answer, "Hi, bird!" Then the canaries would start singing. The commotion would signal to the cats that it was breakfast time, and all four of them would begin racing from room to room, frantically meowing as they anticipated their first meal of the day. How had I slept through all the morning excitement? I eased back the covers and slowly sat up on the edge of the bed. Next to my empty teacup, I saw a handwritten note on the nightstand: "Stay in bed. Or else." I smiled at Peter's humor.

I would have liked to stay in bed. I knew my body well enough, and it had officially reached the point of exhaustion. I was mentally fatigued, physically run down, and heartsick over the loss of Mathilda and all the other sugar gliders. And then there was Marnie's surprise announcement that she'd been offered another job. I couldn't take anymore.

Last night, after I'd dissolved into sobs at the kitchen table in front of Luke and Peter, I'd gone upstairs and collapsed. Peter had discovered me an hour later in a wasted heap on the bed. I'd looked up at him through salty slits for eyes and divulged the grim details of how I'd lost Mathilda, my fifth baby glider, and that my best friend and colleague was, in another way, leaving me too.

"I'm so sorry." Peter had kissed me on the forehead and pulled a blanket over my limp body. "Get some rest," he'd said and gone downstairs to make me some tea.

In the morning light, I read his note again. If it were another day, I probably would take Peter's advice to stay in bed, but I just couldn't. I had to rally. I'd lost too many lives. How many more animals would become sick and perhaps even die on my examination table before I could determine the source of this mysterious illness?

I stood up and felt a light-headed rush of disorientation. I staggered and sat down. *Maybe I'll just lie back down for five more minutes.* I collapsed onto the pillows and closed my eyes.

Bean, joined by Bingo and Gizmo, jumped up on the bed and stretched out beside me like a patchwork quilt. As I floated into that fuzzy haze just before you fall asleep, I thought back to the Central Park turtle I'd treated.

I was filling in for a resident doctor at the Animal Medical Center in New York City when I answered a call from the Midtown police. A huge snapping turtle had crawled out of the Central Park Turtle Pond at 79th Street and made his way all the way over to West 81st Street and Columbus Avenue, where a car had hit him as he had attempted to cross the street. I knew the intersection well, and it was always clogged with traffic.

"We think it might have been a taxi," the officer said, "but we can't be sure since there weren't any witnesses."

"How big is he?" I was curious.

"About seventy pounds, I'd guess, which makes us wonder how any driver could have missed him. Unless it was a taxi," he added. "They'll do anything to make a light."

I silently agreed. I'd suffered my share of scrapes and bruises while the meter was running. Once I'd been sent headfirst into the plastic partition between the front and back seats when the driver stopped abruptly after flooring it through a yellow light.

"Can we bring him in?" the police officer asked about the turtle. "He's pretty, well . . . he's pretty messed up."

"I can treat him medically, but if he survives he'll need a licensed wildlife rehabilitator to further treat him before he returns to his home in the pond," I said.

"Well, right now what he needs most is someone who can put Humpty Dumpty back together again."

"Bring him in," I said, wondering what I'd agreed to.

Hugo, as I found out he was named, was a common snapping turtle whose upper shell was at least three feet long and just as wide. But by the time he arrived at the Animal Medical Center in a crunched-up heap, I thought he looked more like a prehistoric puzzle with a few pieces missing. Every part of his exterior body seemed to have been hurt by the accident. Both his carapace and his plastron, the upper and lower parts of his shell, respectively, looked as if they had been crushed by a wrecking ball, and his jaw was broken in so many places that it distorted his face. It was hard to recognize where his mouth was exactly.

"Where do we start?" asked Dave, my intern at the Center.

With his shell so fragmented, I really didn't know. I was amazed that any animal in this condition could still be alive. Hugo tilted his head in my direction and slowly blinked his huge, sad eyes. He seemed to be asking me for help. I thought, what am I going to do with your poor shell? I needed *The User's Manual to Reassembling Broken Turtles*, but as far as I knew, a guide like that didn't exist. So I pulled on a pair of gloves, injected a mild tranquilizer into one of his legs, and began by carefully examining him from head to tail. His jaw was definitely broken, and his shell was in pieces, but thankfully he didn't appear to have suffered any major internal injuries. He was breathing normally, he was able to move his limbs when I prodded him, and his gums were a healthy pink color, indicating that he hadn't lost a dangerous amount of blood.

I concluded that Hugo's broken jaw was the first thing that would need fixing since he'd need to be able to eat properly to recover. Since the procedure would involve passing needles threaded with wire through the fragments of bone and placing screws and nuts through some of the larger fragments of his jaw, I would have to anesthetize him fully. Like any animal, reptiles feel pain, so I gave the poor crushed turtle a sedative and a painkiller and then passed a large breathing tube down his trachea to hook up the gas anesthesia. Dave and I monitored his breathing and heart rate carefully, and I began the meticulous process of screwing and wiring the fragments of Hugo's broken jaw back together as if it were a broken piece of antique china.

Once Hugo's jaw was wired together and his vitals were stable, I began the laborious job of piecing back together his enormous shell. After all, a turtle is nothing without its shell, which is actually a living piece of bone covered with hard keratin plates, and Hugo would need his to be intact before he could return to the Central Park Turtle Pond. The question was, what would be strong enough to hold his shell together permanently so that it could withstand being in the water again? Surgical glue works fine on soft tissue, but on a turtle shell it wouldn't do. Hugo needed a permanent and solid fix. It came to me in a flash: acrylic and epoxy. The stuff holds planes and ships together. The only problem: epoxy isn't commonly kept in the medicine cabinet.

"Dave! Can you run an errand for me?"

"Sure. What do you want me to pick up? Coffee?"

"Something stronger. Run to the hardware store down the street and pick up epoxy and liquid acrylic."

He arched his eyebrows. "Satin, matte, or gloss?"

To re-create the most authentic turtle shell look, a faux finish in crackle would have been ideal, but since I was going for functionality rather than aesthetic appeal, I said, "It really doesn't matter. Whatever they have."

Twenty minutes later, I had the materials in hand. I cleaned out all the cracks in Hugo's shell with surgical scrub, making sure they were as free of debris as possible—not the easiest task, given that the animal resided in a stagnant pond in Central Park and had just been run over with tire tread. I got him as clean as I could, and then I mixed the five-minute epoxy and layered it over small pieces of fiberglass mesh that bridged the cracks in the shell, joining them back together piece by piece.

When I finished, Hugo's face and shell were covered in wire, but at least he resembled a turtle. We turned down the anesthesia, and finally Hugo opened his eyes.

"I think it's going to hold," I said to Dave, "but it's going to take time."

I traced the jagged lines where I'd glued Hugo's shell back together. The epoxy would need hours, if not days, to set and harden. In his current state Hugo was too fragile to return to the Central Park Turtle Pond. But I didn't have enough room in the clinic to rehabilitate a seventy-two-pound snapping turtle. I left Hugo in the surgery room and called Chris, a veterinary technician friend of mine in the neighboring upstate town of Katonah, who was an excellent reptile rehabilitator. He would know what to do.

As I'd hoped, Chris said he'd be more than happy to treat Hugo—under one condition: I'd have to keep him overnight and deliver him to Katonah myself in the morning.

"I won't have space for him until then," he apologized.

"No problem," I said, not wanting to sound unappreciative, although I didn't really have space for Hugo at the center either. I hung up the phone and considered the situation. Katonah was an hour's drive from Manhattan but only a fifteen-minute freeway ride from my home in Mount Kisco. There was really only one option.

I sent Dave back to the hardware store for a big plastic tub. Together, we filled the bottom with water, lined the bottom of my Toyota Highlander with newspaper, and hoisted the makeshift pool into the back of my car. Just like that, my car was transformed into a giant reptile tank.

On the count of three, Dave and I hoisted Hugo into the back of my car as though we were deadlifting weight in a CrossFit class. Plop! He landed in the tub with a thud. Not the most graceful patient restraint I'd performed but enough to accomplish our goal. I jumped into the front seat and cranked up the heat so that Hugo wouldn't catch cold. Reptiles need extra heat, especially when they're sick or in recovery.

I made my way toward FDR drive to the RFK Bridge. With every slight turn and bump along the way, water splashed as Hugo slid from side to side in the tub like a boulder. I took the Sprain Brook Parkway, and after I made it onto the Saw Mill River Parkway an hour later, I slowed down considerably and put my hazards on. I didn't want to further upset Hugo after all he'd been through today: car accident, jaw surgery, and shell reconstruction. I stayed in the right lane, and we crept along like that for several miles until I saw red lights flash behind me, followed by the quick blast of a siren. Fantastic, I muttered to myself. Another obstacle in the road. I pulled over and waited for the officer to approach.

"Good evening, ma'am. I noticed you have your hazards on. Is everything okay?"

"No problem, really. I'm transporting an injured turtle to a wildlife rehabilitator. He's rather large. That's why I'm driving so slow."

The officer looked perplexed so I clarified, "I'm a vet. An animal doctor."

"Oh, okay," he said, "that makes a little more sense. Do you mind if I take a look?"

We walked to the back of the car, and I lifted up the hatch.

The police officer took a few steps back in alarm. "Jesus, that's a turtle?"

Hugo looked up at the police officer and opened his mouth as if to say hello, revealing a Frankenstein display of bolts, screws, and wires. "He doesn't much look like it, but yes, he's from the Central Park Turtle Pond," I assured him. "He decided to take a walk in Manhattan today and was hit by a car. Trust me, he looked a lot worse a few hours ago."

"I can't imagine," he said and promptly closed the hatch. "Given the unusual circumstances I won't ticket you, but please do your best to drive the speed limit, okay, Doctor?"

It took us nearly two hours, but we finally arrived home. I was in the garage, attempting to lift Hugo's tub out of the car by myself and with the last grain of strength I had, when I heard a little voice behind me.

"Mommy?"

I turned around to find five-year-old Brett standing in his pajamas, wearing an astonished expression.

"Why is there a dinosaur in the garage?"

"This is Hugo," I said. "He's a snapping turtle who was in an accident, but Mommy put him back together again."

His eyes widened further. "Can I bring him to school for show and tell?"

Hugo spent one night in a safe and secure plastic tub filled with a few inches of water inside our garage. I rigged up a heat lamp to ensure that he would be warm enough overnight and also to allow his skin to soak up some ultraviolet light, necessary for turtles and tortoises to make enough vitamin D to enable them to absorb calcium from their food. Brett accompanied me to check on Hugo several times before I declared it "bedtime" for both little boys and turtles.

The next morning I drove Hugo to Katonah and turned him over to a seasoned team of reptile rehabilitators for rest and rehab. After several months, the hardware was removed from Hugo's face and shell, and he was returned to the Central Park Turtle Pond. His recovery was even celebrated in the *New York Post*. The headline read, "Prehistoric Central Park Turtle Rescued and Repaired!"

I hadn't thought about Hugo for years, but now the memory filled me with renewed strength to open my eyes and face the day. Mathilda's death had been devastating, and the thought of Marnie leaving filled me with a dreaded sense of finality. We'd been there for each other through the births of our kids and the deaths of pets and relatives. We'd supported each other unquestioningly for over a decade. What would I do without her? Over the years I've consoled countless pet owners who've lost their closest and most cherished companions. In the heart of their grief, many have told me that their years with their pets outweighed their suffering now. I knew this was true, having loved and lost pets of my own. The risk of developing deep bonds that may one day be stretched, compromised, or even broken is worth the hurt and the pain. I took a deep breath and sat up in bed. I'll get through this. I'll put myself back together again. Just like Hugo. Piece by piece.

And anyway, Marnie was only going to LA.

I threw on my favorite yoga pants and a T-shirt and plodded downstairs. After a bowl of chicken noodle soup and a cup of green tea, I gave in and took a cold tablet. The recommended dose is two, but I usually take the child's dosage of one on account of my small size. Peter likes to tease me about that, and I always make the point, "Hey, this way the bottle lasts us twice as long."

I positioned myself at the kitchen table and opened my laptop. A stack of unopened mail was waiting for me, mostly more disgruntled protests in response to my statements online. I groaned. Just wait until news of Mathilda's death gets out, I thought, and then I recoiled at the thought of the same TV reporter from the Johnson Valley Mall showing up at my hospital for an interview. What would I tell him? How long could I continue to defend Sugar Buddies? How many more of Simon's gliders would fall sick before I identified the source of illness? I was praying for a miracle when my hospital cell phone rang. It was Marnie.

"Why aren't you here? Are you okay?" She sounded both frustrated and concerned.

"I'm not avoiding you, if that's what you're wondering. I overslept, and I'm not feeling so hot, but I'm on my way."

"Well, you better get in here. Quickly. I think we may finally have a break in the case."

"What? How?" I quickened and suddenly revived.

"An Amazon parrot arrived at the hospital about an hour ago. He's thirty-five years old, and his owner brought him in weak and shaking. I initially thought he was suffering from gout, as we see so often in older birds, so Colette and I ran an in-hospital blood test to check his kidneys. Since he also has dark red urine"—the telltale sign of lead poisoning in parrots—"we decided to check his lead level too."

We often have to test and treat parrots for lead toxicity, as they have a habit of chewing on anything they can sink their beaks into.

"And?"

"The lead reading came back high."

I wasn't following. "What does any of this have to do with the sick gliders?"

"Laurie, the symptoms the Amazon is exhibiting are exactly the same as what we've seen in the gliders—weakness, tremors and shaking, dehydration, decreased appetite, inability to climb."

Lead poisoning? Could it be that lead was the cause of all the glider deaths? I took a moment and turned this over in my mind. The signs and symptoms of the sick gliders were in fact similar to those we see in birds with lead toxicity. But lead poisoning doesn't spread from animal to animal, and Simon's gliders were sick all over the country. At what point would all of the sick gliders have been exposed to toxic lead? I still couldn't connect the dots. Where was the lead coming from?

As I considered this, I asked Marnie, "Any ideas how the Amazon parrot was exposed?"

"His owner thinks it may have been from an old metal bell in his cage. Possibly lead in the paint. The bell's been in the cage for years, he said, but the bird never bothered with it until about two weeks ago when the Amazon took a sudden interest, and his owner says he's been chewing on it night and day. You should see it. The parrot's scraped all the outer coating off the outside of the bell, and the clapper is nearly gone."

Lead poisoning from the metal bell was entirely plausible. Some of the older metal toys, especially those manufactured overseas, contain toxic lead in the paint and sometimes in the metal itself, which can slowly chip off or leach out if an animal repeatedly chews on it. My mind flipped back to the sick gliders. When would any of Simon's young gliders have been exposed to old metal toys? Most all of the new pet toys on the market are lead-free and also BPA-, PVC-, and phthalate-free. The pet toy aisle in PetSmart or Petco these days looks similar to the newborn section in Babies"R"Us. Nearly everything is marked with a safety sticker. Still, I couldn't dispute the connection Marnie had made—there was no denying their shared symptoms. All of the gliders I'd lost had exhibited similar signs to the hundreds of birds I'd treated for lead toxicity over the course of my career. Although a very low level of lead in the blood is generally not harmful, when the lead concentration reaches a critical threshold, the metal can start to interfere with organ function and can cause anemia, weakness, and ultimately death.

"I'll be there in ten minutes." I threw on my jacket and practically ran out the door.

ON THE DRIVE to the hospital I recalled the last time I'd treated an Amazon parrot for lead poisoning. It was 11:30 p.m. on a Sunday night, and my phone went off. It was a text message from the answering service: "Mrs. Hurvitz in Peekskill, NY, calling about her 26-year-old Amazon parrot, Morris. Please call ASAP." I dialed her number and heard a frantic woman at the other end crying. "Dr. Hess, Dr. Hess . . . it's Morris. He got his foot stuck in the metal chain of a toy hanging in his cage when I was out, and I came home to find him dangling by his toes. He must have been hanging there for hours trying to free himself, because I found him upside down, having chewed one of his toes off. He also seems to have bitten off parts of the metal chain. I freed him from the toy, but he has lost a lot of blood."

"I'll meet you at the hospital in fifteen minutes," I said.

As I zoomed into the parking lot, I spotted Debra Hurvitz already standing outside the hospital waiting for me. I unlocked the door, disarmed the alarm, and showed her immediately into an exam room. I took Morris, a big green-and-yellow Amazon parrot, out of his carrier. Indeed, he had a bloody stump where one of his toes should have been. It was no longer actively bleeding, but Morris was pale and lethargic. Normally, he was an active and noisy bird, often squawking and flapping his wings as I examined him.

Morris had been a patient of mine for years, and I loved seeing Debra as we always had something in common to chat about. The last time I had seen the pair, about a year before, Debra had shared with me her excitement that she'd finally left the corporate world in New York City to follow her dream of opening her own ice cream store in a nearby town in my area of upstate New York. I'd just read an article in the local paper about how successful her artisan ice creamery had become.

I cleaned and bandaged Morris's mangled toe as Debra attempted to hold him steady for me. I administered a painkiller and an antibiotic injection, as well as a shot of iron and some fluids underneath his skin. I told Debra that he would be okay and to keep him quiet in his cage overnight and come back in

Monday morning. Debra hugged me profusely and promised to be on my doorstep first thing in the morning. Sure enough, like clockwork, she was there at the stroke of 9 a.m., as Marnie and I simultaneously pulled into the parking lot to open the hospital for the day.

I was delighted to see that Morris's color had returned and he was back to his usual squawky self. He'd chewed a little on his bandage, but his toe was still covered, and the inside of his mouth was no longer pale. Debra pulled an old, rusty, chipped metal chain from her purse. "I forgot to show you this last night," she commented.

I examined the chain: all the links were intact, but Morris had chewed through the outer coating on the metal, likely as he tried to free his toes from the toy.

"Wow, he must have been really frustrated," I responded, turning the chain over in my hand. "I'm a little concerned, based on the age of this toy and the amount Morris chewed, that he may have ingested lead or zinc. I think we should test him for these metals."

Marnie and I took blood from Morris and loaded it into the lead machine in our lab. A few minutes later, out came the report: high. We immediately started treatment with an injectable metal chelation medication, and I gave Debra the oral version to administer to Morris at home.

Debra replaced all of the old toys in his cage with new, lead-free toys and brought Morris back for a follow-up measurement of his lead level a week later. That time, the reading came back normal. Before leaving the hospital, she presented Marnie and me with an insulated cooler bag containing three pints of homemade ice cream—Birdie Banana,

Pineapple Parrot, and Raspberry Rabbit, the fruity flavors in her store named for the types of pets she kept. To this day, this thank-you gesture stands out as one of the more delicious gifts I've ever received.

11:12 A.M., ANIMAL HOSPITAL

I THREW OPEN the hospital doors and made a beeline through the waiting room. I greeted Colette with a rushed "Morning."

"Good morning," she said, looking me up and down. "Did you run here?"

"Huh?" I looked down and realized that in my mad dash to leave the house, I'd forgotten to change out of my Athleta wear and Nike sneakers. Instead of stopping to explain, I said, "Sure." Sometimes the best answer is the simplest one, even if it's not necessarily the truth.

I found Marnie in the emergency care area treating the lead-poisoned Amazon parrot with calcium EDTA injections while simultaneously trying to run a blood test on Lily.

"Just in time," she said. "Colette's been busy up at the front desk, and I need help restraining Lily so I can get a blood sample from her leg. I tried to do it alone, but I'm just not that coordinated, and I don't want to make her any more uncomfortable than she already is."

Without a specific blood test, it's impossible to confirm the presence of lead in the body, let alone lead poisoning. I hadn't ordered the test or performed anything other than a broad blood panel on any of the sick gliders because I'd never once treated, or ever even heard of, an instance of a sugar glider being poisoned with the neurotoxic metal. The routine blood count and chemistry tests I had performed on each animal had revealed mild anemia and slight elevation in kidney function values, which are consistent with the presence of lead, but those irregularities can also be attributed to any number of diseases. The possibility that the sugar gliders were suffering from lead poisoning never entered my mind.

I cradled Lily's tiny, frail body in a towel on the treatment table as Marnie extended her back leg to identify the hairlike vein that ran just above her ankle. She dabbed Lily's leg with an alcohol-soaked cotton ball to make the vein more visible, and as I held pressure on her leg above the vein to make it stand up, Marnie gently inserted the almost invisibly thin 33-gauge needle—the kind I use to administer insulin to myself—into the vein. We needed just a drop or two of blood to check for lead; in fact, that's often all we can get from our small patients. Marnie got the sample, and we whisked it to our lab and loaded it into the lead analyzer.

Blood lead levels are measured on analyzers that detect the concentration of lead in the bloodstream. Many veterinary hospitals don't have these special machines and must send blood samples out to laboratories for analysis. But given how often we see lead poisoning in birds, I had bitten the lead bullet, so to speak, and bought an in-hospital machine. Having to wait days to get lead test results back can sometimes mean the difference between life and death for a bird, so having the in-hospital lead-testing machine, which gave us results within minutes, had saved many lives.

I held my breath for what seemed like an eternity until the lead analyzer whirred to a stop.

Marnie said, "Take a look at this."

The word "high" appeared on the machine's screen, indicating that Lily's blood contained lead at a level too high for the machine to actually measure.

I looked at Marnie in disbelief, but the test was definitive. "You're right."

My mind rewound over the past week of events, scrambling to put the pieces of the puzzle together. Could lead exposure have caused the premature deaths of Mathilda, Georgie, Pockets, and all the other young gliders in Westchester County and across the country? I recalled Georgie's necropsy report. On my urging, our chief pathologist in California had rushed the organ sample results back to me in two days. I hadn't recognized anything in her report that suggested the presence of lead. But again, lead won't be identified directly without a specific test for its presence. The pathologist had identified changes in several different organ systems, including degeneration and necrosis of liver and kidney cells, as well as segmental demyelination of nerves. Thinking about it now, demyelination is a characteristic lesion seen with lead poisoning, although it can also appear with inflammation from other causes. I'd read her full report, and not seeing anything new or that appeared inconsistent with my findings so far, I'd tossed it on top of Georgie's paperwork to file away later.

But now, when I considered the necropsy report again, I realized Georgie might very well have suffered from lead toxicity. I reworked the case in my head: young gliders, all weak and dying, from different geographic locations, with minimal to no response to supportive treatments—and, now it appeared, all exhibiting symptoms consistent with lead poisoning

"Start an aggressive treatment of oral dimercaptosuccinic acid with repeated calcium EDTA injections, large doses of subcutaneous fluid, oral Epsom salts to absorb lead, and syringe feeding. We need to also run a lead test on Baby G."

Since I'd brought Baby G into the hospital, he hadn't exhibited any signs of sickness; nor had any of the routine tests detected any abnormalities in his system. He was wide-eyed and curious, unable to sit still, actually, and climbing up and down the sides of his cage, curious to assess his new environment. Whenever I opened his cage, he did what all normal, healthy sugar gliders do: he leapt into the air, opened his arms wide, and glided onto the front of my lab coat, digging his nails into the fabric to secure a landing. For all appearances, Baby G was as healthy as he should be. And still, I acknowledged now, his display of active behavior didn't discount exposure to or ingestion of lead. Many animals don't start showing clinical signs of illness until their blood lead level reaches a critical threshold, which can vary from animal to animal. It was possible that he had been exposed to lead but hadn't ingested enough of the metal to produce symptoms, or even signs, of toxicity. Only a lead test would determine if he had even a trace amount of lead in his system. I took a deep breath, knowing that if the baby glider had even a slightly elevated blood lead level, the source of lead exposure would again point back to Simon's farm.

I retrieved the tiny glider from the intensive care cage and set him down on the main treatment table, under a big overhead surgical light. Getting a blood sample from this tiny animal would be even harder than it had been from Lily. I feared that the veins in his limbs were too slight and narrow to get a large enough sample to enable lead testing. We'd have to anesthetize him and use a very small needle to pull blood from his vena cava, the large blood vessel that drains into

the heart. Just thinking about performing the delicate procedure made me anxious. The risk of lacerating the vena cava
with the needle was considerable, and with even the least
nick, Baby G could bleed to death. To avoid this dreaded
outcome, we'd need to keep him perfectly still throughout
the procedure.

I said to Marnie, "Let's get set up for a vena cava stick on
Baby G."

Without hesitating, Marnie put a mask over his sweet little face to administer the anesthesia. The little glider curled
up agreeably, his tiny head relaxed in the mask, and within a
minute he was groggy and still enough for me to insert the
hairlike 33-gauge insulin needle just above his breastbone into
his chest near his heart. I said a silent prayer: *Don't move a muscle,
little one, stay with me.* I saw blood flow up into the hub of the
needle, and when Baby G took his next small breath, I finally
exhaled myself.

2:30 P.M.

THREE HOURS AFTER Marnie had begun treating Lily with
a combination of oral dimercaptosuccinic acid and Epsom
salts, injected calcium EDTA, and subcutaneous fluids, Bob's
longtime companion started to come back to life. With every passing minute, she showed more promising signs of
improvement.

"This is truly amazing," Marnie said, giddy with relief.

I offered Lily a wedge of sweet potato through the bars of
her cage. She hastened over to retrieve it. Still a bit weak on
her back legs, she stumbled backward and fell over with a plop.

"Easy, girl."

That Lily was recovering right before my eyes was unquestionable. It was what I'd been hoping and praying for. Still, I couldn't quite piece it together. From the lead test, it was definitely clear that Bob's older glider had been exposed to lead, but when—and where? Not on Simon's farm. Lily was the one sick glider I'd treated who I knew absolutely hadn't been born and weaned there. And now, I held the results of Baby G's blood test in my hand. It was negative for lead. Baby G's body held no trace of the toxin. This further suggested that Simon's farm, at least, was likely not the source of exposure. This would relieve him, and yet there were still the mall kiosks and other aspects of the operation to consider. I couldn't draw any more conclusions until another glider tested positive for lead.

"I need to call Hannah," I announced to Marnie, "and ask her to run a lead test on her glider from Winslow Mall."

I JOINED ELLIOT for lunch in the back boarding room. He was watching cartoons with Chloe the rabbit. In between bites of chicken salad, I checked my phone like an obsessive teenager. "It's been over an hour," I groaned. "When's she going to text me back?"

Elliot laughed at me and reached a hand into Chloe's cage. He tenderly scratched her floppy ears. "I've made a decision," he said, distracting me for the moment. "I've decided to adopt another cockatiel."

"What about Scarlet?" I said with a mouthful of salad.

"She's going back with me to Rhode Island. The cockatiel is for my mom and dad. I hadn't realized how much they'd bonded with her when I was away at school and how much they miss her now. They still have her empty cage hanging in the living room. And Mom's got a picture of her taped to the fridge."

"Oh, that's sad but sweet," I said. "Trixie was such a sunny delight. Do you need help finding another cockatiel?"

Before Elliot could answer, we were interrupted by the buzz of my phone with a text message.

"The results of the lead test!" I blurted.

Hannah had responded with one single word, leaving no room for question or interpretation: positive.

There it was, confirmed. The glider adopted from Winslow Mall was also positive for lead. I'd now made a definitive connection between at least two of Simon's gliders sold at two different locations, the Johnson Valley and Winslow Malls. The when and where of exposure were still very much a question mark, but the cause—lead poisoning—was solid.

"Send out an alert on Vets Connect," I said to Elliot, "and if any vet currently treating a sick glider calls the hospital, especially in those cities where Exotic Essentials distributes, tell them they should immediately test for lead. If the reading comes back high, advise them to treat them as they would any animal positive for lead exposure. They should start injectable lead chelation with calcium EDTA to bind up lead in the bloodstream and then send the animal home on oral lead chelation with dimercaptosuccinic acid. The animal's kidney and liver values need to be monitored too, with blood testing to ensure that no additional medical treatment is necessary, and of course any affected animal should be given supportive care with syringe feeding and fluids if it isn't eating on his own."

"Will do," said Elliot as he packed up his lunch.

I added, "If anyone has questions about the source of lead exposure, be sure to emphasize we still don't know what that is. For now, we just want to get the word out before any more animals are lost." Elliot and I hurriedly left the boarding room and sped off in opposite directions. I was nearing the waiting room when I heard Colette sternly say, "Doctor Hess is unavailable for comment right now."

"Well, we want to know why this hospital is supporting an abusive company," a woman argued back. "She said on Facebook they haven't done anything wrong, but we saw the TV report that says they're making animals sick."

Dang social media, I thought as my stomach tightened. I hoped these weren't the voices of protesters like Hannah had encountered at her hospital in Long Island. The critical emails and phone calls were bad enough. I reluctantly turned the corner to discover a woman and her teenage daughter standing shoulder to shoulder in the waiting room.

"I'm Dr. Laurie Hess. Can I help you?"

The woman stepped forward. "My daughter and I are here to protest the abuse of sugar gliders in the region. Live animals should not be sold at mall kiosks like cell phone covers or handbags."

"A shopping mall is not a home," her daughter chimed in.

"I appreciate your concern for these animals, and let me assure you that this hospital does not condone abusive practices. I've dedicated my whole life to caring for exotic pets, and I take very seriously my responsibility to make sure that any animal admitted under my care is not harmed or abused. I don't believe Sugar Buddies is doing either."

"Well then why are the animals dying?" accused the teenage girl.

Her mother looked at her proudly and shot back at me, "Yes, why are they dying, doctor?"

"That's an important question, and I assure you I'm working closely with the company that sets up the adoptions, along with other vets and pathologists across the country, to determine the cause of illness and death and to prevent additional ones."

"And have you?" asked the woman.

I really wanted to say that I thought I had, but until I could determine how Simon's gliders were coming into contact with lead, I couldn't say a thing. "Not yet," I apologized.

"That's what I thought," the woman sneered, then took her daughter by the arm. "Let's go, honey."

Once the dissenting mother-daughter duo were back in their car, I turned to Colette, "If anyone else comes in carrying a protest sign, tell them what I just told those two."

"Got it."

I pulled my phone out of my lab coat and dialed Simon.

"I have news. We've identified the cause of the illness in at least two of your gliders."

"Really," he said eagerly. "What is it?"

I didn't hesitate. "They appear to be suffering from lead poisoning."

"Lead?" Simon questioned. "How? From where?"

"That's what I'm hoping you can tell me. I still haven't determined the source of exposure. All I know for sure is that one of your gliders adopted from Winslow Mall has tested positive for lead. Another glider I'm currently treating at the hospital has also tested positive for lead. She's not one of yours, but she was brought in with a baby glider adopted from Johnson Valley Mall."

"Is that one positive for lead too?"

I paused. "Unfortunately, she died yesterday at my hospital before I could test her for lead exposure."

Simon drew in a deep breath. "And what about the baby you took from my farm? Is he testing positive?"

"No," I lightened. "He tested negative for the toxin, which leads me to believe that—"

Simon exhaled, "They're not being exposed on my farm."

"Most probably not. At this point, that's a viable conclusion, but we can't really conclude anything—absolutely—yet."

"Lead poisoning?" Simon said again after a moment of thought. "You're sure?"

"I am. The blood tests show high levels of lead toxicity with no room for doubt."

"So now what?"

"We look for anywhere those baby gliders of yours are coming into contact with the metal."

"Where do we start?"

"Let's start with the possibility of exposure on the trucks," I said. "When the gliders are loaded onto the trucks, they're housed in transport cages, right?"

"That's right."

"Who supplies these cages?"

"I do."

"Do you know what they're made of? The reason I ask is that we only started testing the gliders for high levels of lead after an Amazon parrot showed up at the hospital with lead poisoning. He'd been chewing on an old metal toy in his cage. We noticed that the symptoms of the sick parrot and the sick gliders were nearly identical. Sugar gliders similarly love to suck, chew on, and use their teeth to climb their cages. If your gliders are chewing on wires that contain lead, then—"

"All our cages are made of stainless steel," Simon cut in. "And they're brand new."

"And do you use the same stainless steel cages on all the transport trucks that leave the farm?"

"Every one. We've been using the same cage supplier for years, and we've never had a problem with them."

"Okay," I said. "What about the water on the trucks? Any chance the tanks are contaminated? Are the animals exposed to water at any point that may be running through old contaminated pipes?"

Simon thought about it. "I fill the water tanks on the trucks myself with the well water I use on the farm. It's the same water I drink. I have the water quality tested twice a year for contaminants—nitrates, bacteria, pesticides. I pay a private lab to do to it, and it costs me a near fortune."

"Do they test for lead?"

"They do—in the well and in the plumbing in the old farmhouse. Reports are always clean. One spring the well flooded after a major rainstorm hit us, and we worried about contaminants from the runoff, but the tests came back clean then too. The farm isn't at all as rural as it used to be; the watershed has been sewered for at least a decade."

"Okay, then," I ruminated, "back to the trucks. Could there be lead in any of their feeding bowls? Is their food stored in any potentially lead-contaminated containers?"

"Nope." I could almost hear Simon shaking his head. "Everything we use is stainless steel, and for that reason—it's the safest material."

"Alright," I said mentally shifting gears. "Let's walk through the possibility of lead exposure at the mall kiosks."

Simon sighed. "I can't think of anything I saw at Winslow Mall that would be exposing them to lead either. The animals come straight off the trucks in the same cages they were transported in and they stay in those cages until they're adopted and go home with their new owners."

"Are the animals sent home with anything that might contain lead? Any chew toys?"

"No, we don't send them home with toys. We do supply new owners with a take-home starter kit that includes a bag of pelleted food, some vitamins and a calcium supplement, a BPA-free plastic water bottle, and specific instructions on glider care."

"None of those things would contain lead," I mumbled to myself. I sank back in my chair. We were getting nowhere—again. I picked up the list of distribution points on my desk and studied it for what felt like the hundredth time. My eyes scanned the list and settled on the scribbling in the margin—the scattering of cities that didn't have a yellow mark through them. The locations that were, so far, immune.

"Wait a minute," I said slowly. "The gliders that are transported to Miami, Chicago, Detroit, Tulsa, and St. Louis—so far, none of the gliders adopted from these locations have become sick or died. What if"—I was thinking out loud now—"we assume that those animals have not been exposed to lead whereas the gliders in the other locations have." I paused and turned it over in my mind.

"Then?" asked Simon.

"Then there must be some variation in their care. Simon, can you think of anything particular about how the baby gliders that go to these locations are transported or sold? Anything at all?"

"I'll make some calls."

WHILE SIMON MADE his calls, I made mine.

"Lead poisoning?" Bob said after a moment of silence.

"We put Lily on calcium EDTA and fluids all morning, and you just won't believe it until you see her with your own eyes. Bob, she's actually jumping around her cage." I started to tear up, thinking about her miraculous transformation.

"Are you certain? I don't want to get my hopes up. Yesterday," he paused, "yesterday was really tough." His voice dropped to a near whisper.

"I promise not to put you through that again. Lily's not dying. She's going to be okay."

Bob must have broken every speed limit between his shop and the hospital, because he came flying through the doors in practically less time than it takes me to check my blood sugar.

Tears welled up in his eyes, too, as soon as he saw Lily climbing the walls of her intensive care cage. I opened the small door, and she leapt into the air and landed on his chest. He scooped her up and held her close. Lily looked up at Bob with black, jellybean eyes, and he touched the tip of her pink nose with his own. "You really scared me," he cried. "I thought I was going to lose you, too, and what would I do without my best girl?" Lily wrapped her long dark tail around Bob's wrist, as if to comfort him and securely set anchor.

He snuggled her for as long as she could stay still. Then she let out a joyful squeak and scampered up Bob's arm. Before

I registered what was happening, she launched into the air and landed on top of my head.

Bob laughed. "Oh, there she goes. I'm sorry, Doctor. Let me get her."

"I'm used to this." I reached up and retrieved her from my nest of curls. "Plus, I've never been so happy to have an animal in my hair."

Her movement proved to me that her back legs were regaining their strength and that she was recovering faster than I could have hoped for.

I handed Lily back to Bob. "I think she's ready to go home."

As I prepared Lily for release from the hospital, writing up instructions for her in-home care, I continued to sneak looks at Bob and Lily's sweet reunion. I interrupted their back-and-forth play only to advise, "Monitor her appetite and energy level, and ensure that she's eating. You may need to hand-feed or syringe-feed her until she's eating well enough on her own again. If she begins to show any indication that she's lethargic or weak or if her appetite decreases, call me immediately."

"Of course I'll call if anything seems off." Bob said as Lily broke free of his grasp and scampered up his arm. Bob playfully caught her before she made it to his shoulder.

"Gotcha."

"Other than that," I said, watching them, "just enjoy each other."

It was clear to me that Bob and Lily had made the same unspoken promise I'd observed between countless pet owners and their pets over the years: unwavering devotion. Even when they're sick or challenging or when they simply inconvenience or frustrate us, we make an agreement with our pets to stand by them, no matter what. I considered that this

same understanding extends to our human friendships too. I
thought about Marnie and our bond and how, even if she left
the hospital for another job, I'd support her absolutely. Our
friendship would endure wherever we were because of the unspoken agreement we'd made with each other over the years,
again and again, to never let go.

I remembered seven-year-old Sam Ellison, who had made
the same promise with his pet, Robbie, a lop-eared rabbit I'd
treated a couple of years ago.

"There has to be something you can do. Sam can't lose his
best buddy. Not now."

We were standing just outside the examination room, and I
followed Mrs. Ellison's gaze down the hallway to the waiting
room, where her son sat quietly looking through the holiday
classic *Stranger in the Woods*. Though I never want to give anyone a difficult diagnosis, sometimes it has to be done. The
hard truth was that Sam's lop-eared rabbit had thymoma, a
tumor in the chest cavity that can be very hard to treat. It
would require more than a simple biopsy and removal. Radi-
ation treatment would likely be required to shrink the tumor,
and maybe even surgery would be needed to get it all, which
is always risky and expensive and never a guarantee for a cure.

"Since my husband and I separated, Sam won't go anywhere without Robbie. Most of the time, Robbie's the only
one Sam will talk to," Mrs. Ellison said.

In my head, I'd been cycling through treatments and ex-
penses and a questionable prognosis even with the best of attempts, when I snapped back to attention. *The only one he talks
to?* If Mrs. Ellison meant she had a hard time communicating
with her son, I could certainly relate. There are days when
I feel like no matter what I say or how I say it, I still can't

get through to Brett and Luke. Clean up your room. Do your homework. Feed the pets. I repeated the same requests over and over, but the boys seemed to have selective hearing. I was guaranteed a response only when they heard the word "food." But that's how most parents feel, isn't it?

Mrs. Ellison continued sadly, "Everything between his dad and me—it's back and forth, unsettled. We're trying to work it through, but I think Sam feels lost, like nothing's within his control, and his family is falling apart right in front of him. Robbie's his one, true thing that he can depend on. I don't want Sam to lose him too."

My heart pulled toward Sam. "I will do everything I can to help make sure that your son doesn't lose his friend, but," I said honestly, "this is going to be a long process. With or without surgery, treating Robbie will likely involve syringe feeding, medications, fluids, and visits here at least once a week, possibly for several weeks. It's a big-time commitment and a significant expense." And maybe more than Sam's parents could take on, I thought, while also trying to salvage their marriage and tend to their young son.

Mrs. Ellison nodded. "I understand what you're saying, and in a way it makes the most sense to forgo treating Robbie. It would be more convenient, less expensive. One less thing to shoulder right now. But what would that teach Sam? That pets are dispensable? That relationships aren't worth fighting for? Our children listen to us, but more than that, it's what they see us do that they really learn from."

Humbled by her words and their truth, I walked back into the examining room and looked down at Robbie. To treat this sick rabbit, I'd have to begin by placing a catheter is his leg, a breathing tube down his airway, electronic leads on his limbs to measure heart rate, and a temperature probe in his rectum—a lot for the little rabbit to take. I put my hand on the top of Robbie's head and gently stroked his soft, downy ears. He relaxed under my touch, and his breathing steadily slowed down and became more regular. *Hang in there, little guy. Your friend needs you.*

6:00 P.M., DRIVING HOME

I WAS NEARLY home when I answered a call from Simon in the car.

"I just spoke with the chief distributor at Exotic Essentials," he said eagerly. "I told him we were trying to pinpoint possible exposure to lead, and I asked him if he could look into how the mall kiosks were set up in Chicago, Detroit, Tulsa, and St. Louis specifically. Was there anything different, out of the ordinary, or special about how those kiosks are being run. Of course his first response was 'I don't think so,' but he said he'd look into it, make a few calls.

"I started thinking back to what you said about the bird that came into your hospital with lead poisoning from chewing on old metal toys in its cage. That's when it hit me. I can't believe I didn't think of this before."

"What?" I nearly shouted into the phone.

"Like I said earlier, the cages on my transport trucks are all stainless steel. I know this absolutely because I order every single one of them myself from the same supplier I've been using for years. But," Simon paused, "what I don't order is the supply of cages that the adopted gliders go home in."

I stopped short at a red light. My stomach tightened. "What do you mean? What other cages?"

"Remember when I said that the gliders stay in the transport cages *until* they're adopted?"

"Yes."

"Whenever a glider is adopted from a mall kiosk, the new pet is sent home in a 'take-home' cage. They look just like the transport cages, only smaller—about two feet by two feet. All of the gliders adopted from Johnson Valley Mall would have gone home in a cage like this."

"And where do those cages come from?" I asked, holding my breath.

"Exotic Essentials supplies them to all of the mall kiosks throughout the country."

I waited for him to continue, still holding my breath.

"I called the chief distributor back and asked him what he knew about these cages—who makes and supplies them. Did he know what materials they're made from, et cetera." Simon said.

"And?"

"He couldn't answer all my questions, but what he did know was pretty interesting."

"Go on."

"The cages sent home with newly adopted gliders are supplied by different cage manufacturers, depending on geographical location. And according to him, Exotic Essentials recently added a new cage manufacturer to its distribution list, one the company hasn't used before."

My heart was racing. "Does he know where this new order of cages was distributed?"

"He's confirming that now. I'll call you back as soon as I know more."

I couldn't wait that long. I checked my rearview mirror for traffic before making an abrupt U-turn in the middle of the road. As I sped back toward the hospital, I thought back to when Maxine and Mr. Huntington had brought their sick gliders in. I recalled that they'd delivered them in their own travel carriers. But Bob had transported Lily to the hospital in a small wire cage and carried Mathilda in his shirt pocket. At the time, I'd thought this was Bob's clever way to surprise me with his new baby glider. I tried to force the memory. Had he left the cage at the hospital? He hadn't taken Lily home in it yesterday. If he'd left it behind, where was it now?

7:12 P.M., ANIMAL HOSPITAL

I FOUND LILY'S cage in the back storage room on top of a stack of pelleted ferret food. I hauled it down and rummaged around for a First Alert kit in the supply closet. With both in hand, I retreated to the nearest examination room. I'd used these over-the-counter kits before to test for lead on painted surfaces and steel structures before we remodeled our house, and I'd used them sporadically at the hospital to test for lead in metal toys. I removed the swab from the kit and rubbed it along the surface of the cage. I'd found one wire with small indentations, likely from teeth marks. I stood motionless with the swab in my hand and waited. Five, ten, fifteen . . . within seconds, the swab turned red, indicating that lead was present on contact.

I dropped the swab and fumbled for my phone. My fingers were shaking as I dialed Simon's cell.

"It's the transport cages," I said, nearly out of breath. "They contain lead."

IT WAS SEVERAL days before the tests were conclusive. But we eventually discovered that in the cities where newly adopted sugar gliders had become sick and were dying, the take-home cages from the nearby malls were from the new cage supplier. And all of those cages tested positive for a PVC vinyl coating on the cage bars that revealed the presence of lead. Veterinarians treating sick gliders from these mall locations nearly all confirmed moderate to high levels of the toxic metal in the animals' systems. The new supplier maintained it was not aware that the coating on the cage bars would be harmful to the animals, but it took full responsibility for the unfortunate deaths. On the urging of Exotic Essentials, they issued a nationwide recall of its cages and promised to take corrective measures, beginning with testing all of its current inventory for harmful lead in the cage bars. Exotic Essentials also pledged to test all of its cages for the presence of lead, regardless of the cage manufacturer, before issuing them to new owners.

The national sugar glider association issued a statement to the wide veterinary community, identifying the metal as causing the "involuntary tremoring syndrome in sugar gliders" and acknowledging the efforts made by me and Hannah and other veterinarians across the country who tirelessly collated data to help pinpoint the cause of the mysterious illness. The president of the association also recognized Sugar Buddies for being "extremely proactive and supportive of the entire veterinary community in taking the lead in addressing and resolving this unfortunate situation for all affected sugar gliders."

At last Simon was vindicated.

Back at the hospital we continued to populate pet message boards, urging owners of sick gliders to immediately remove the animals from their cages and seek treatment. I also posted the discovery on Vets Connect and encouraged all veterinarians to contact Exotic Essentials directly if they encountered any more gliders with symptoms indicative of lead toxicity—mild tremors, seizures, and partial paralysis. The wide community of veterinarians across the country began similarly to post on their hospitals' social media pages that owners of sick sugar gliders should immediately replace their animals' cages to reduce continued exposure and give their pets a fighting chance.

The scattered distribution of lead-containing cages explained why only a small population of gliders in each mall location had become sick, and only after they were in their new homes. As they're apt to do, the baby gliders began to suck and chew on the coated bars of their cages as soon as they were put into them. Little by little and day by day, they chewed away at the bars, ingesting the toxic metal with every bite. I understood now why in nearly every case of exposure, the animals hadn't begun to show signs of illness until they'd been in their new homes for nearly a week. Lead builds up in the body over time, and animals don't start showing symptoms of toxicity until their blood lead level reaches a certain critical level. This also explained why only the adopted animals became sick. The sugar gliders yet to find new homes remained healthy and safe in Simon's larger, stainless steel truck transport cages. A glider didn't get exposed to lead until it was removed from the larger mall population and placed in a small, take-home cage. Gliders adopted from malls in Chicago, Detroit, Tulsa, and St. Louis were seemingly immune because the cages in those locations came from one of Exotic Essentials' older, trusted suppliers.

I called Bob to explain why Mathilda had died. As always, he was gracious when he didn't need to be.

"I understand now why Lily got sick too."

Bob recalled that when he had first brought Mathilda home from Johnson Valley Mall, he'd moved Lily into the small take-home cage along with the baby glider.

"To keep her company and help her acclimate to her new surroundings."

For several days the two gliders had snuggled together in the small cage and also sucked and chewed on the metal bars that would eventually make them sick.

"After a few days, though," Bob said, "it became clear that they were cramped. The cage was really too tight to house two active gliders, so I moved them both over to Lily's larger cage with its many platforms and perches for them to jump and fly around."

That had been Lily's saving grace. She'd been exposed to lead in the small cage, but not enough to suffer major organ damage. Mathilda, on the other hand, because she was so young and small, was more vulnerable. Even the slightest amount of lead in her system was too much for her body to handle.

In addition to their public pledge to test every cage before it landed in the hands of a new glider owner, Exotic Essentials voluntarily offered to replace any animal that had died with another baby glider, should the owner wish or request one. I appreciated the company's effort to right a wrong, but I also knew well that for most owners, cages are replaceable; their special pets are not. Still, I hoped that Maxine and the many others who had tragically lost their gliders would someday be able to move past their grief and give yet another animal a happy, loving, and safe home, which is all any creature wants.

7

LOVE WITHOUT RESERVATION

THE FOLLOWING SATURDAY, 10:00 A.M., HOME

At last, I was stretched out on the family room couch, sipping a Diet Coke and mindlessly flipping through *Health* magazine. Peter padded into the room in his sweatpants. "Well, look who it is: doctor by day, detective by night. You're not just a DVM anymore. You need to add PI to your list of credentials now." He lowered his voice, pretending to sound like a serious newscaster: "The mysterious deaths of sugar gliders across the country has been solved. Lead poisoning."

I smiled and lightly socked him on the arm as he sank down beside me. It was finally over. I'd lost four too many baby gliders on my examination table, but at least Marnie and I had saved Lily. I could begin to restore balance in the hospital, and life could get back to normal, whatever that was.

Peter propped his feet up on the ottoman, and Dale flew in from the kitchen and perched comfortably on his shoulder. "It's nice to see you finally relax and take a little bit of down time," he said while patting around on the couch cushions for the remote. "How long is this going to last?"

"Five more minutes," I groaned and pulled myself up out of my nest of soft cushions. "I'm going into the hospital—just for a few hours."

"I knew you couldn't sit still for long." Peter turned to Dale and said, "She'll never change." Dale chirped in agreement.

"This is who you married," I smirked as I tossed Peter the remote.

"Yes, it is," Peter said with a tone of playful resignation. "And you still owe me a date night."

"I made reservations at Via Vino at five." I said confidently and then walked out of the room. "Oh, and don't be late," I said over my shoulder.

"Hey, that's my line," Peter called after me as Dale mimicked, "DON'T BE LATE! DON'T BE LATE!"

I had only made it as far as the driveway and was scraping ice off the car windshield when Katherine threw open her front door. I pretended not to see her and dug harder into the ice.

"Good morning," she called out across the lawn with a note of pleasantness I wasn't used to. She cut across her driveway and approached me in mine. "You're a local hero." She smiled and put her hands on her hips.

Flattery was not Katherine's typical approach, and besides—what was she getting at?

"Gilman told me all about it. The big pet mystery you just solved," she said with dramatic affect. "Brett told Gilman about it at practice. Sounds very exciting. Like an episode of *House*, but for animals."

I hesitated for a moment while I stared at her perfectly white teeth.

"Isn't it funny." She laughed at herself, "We've lived right next door to each other for years, and I've never really known what you do. Something to do with animals." She shrugged. "But I didn't realize you were so, you know"—she looked up as if she were searching for the words to fall out of the sky— "well respected."

I smiled coolly. "In some circles."

"Well, anyway," she perked, "since you know so much about animals, I wondered if you could give me some advice about Gilman's pet hamster."

I stopped scraping the ice. Was Katherine actually asking me for parenting advice? Was I hallucinating? "Um, sure," I said with some hesitation.

"He's been begging me for a pet all year, so I finally gave in and got him one."

I thought to myself that a hamster was the type of pet you get for a younger child, not for an eighth grader. In fact, I recommend them often, along with guinea pigs and lizards, as great starter pets for little ones because they're fairly low-maintenance, friendly animals.

"Well, it wasn't *my* choice"—she rolled her eyes—"but Gilman said he'd always wanted one, and since he hasn't gotten as much attention in the house since I've had the baby, I thought, okay, whatever." She shrugged again. "So, now we have a hamster." She lowered her voice and leaned in. "But I don't know the first thing about taking care of an animal like that. When I was little, we had dogs."

Now it was my turn to smile. Katherine wasn't the perfect parent after all, and she was admitting it. I let her request hang in the cool air to fully appreciate the moment before I responded.

"Well, hamsters are pretty easy," I said finally. "They like to keep relatively cool, exercise daily on a wheel, and that's about it. If cared for properly, they can live a long time."

"If cared for properly," she repeated my words back to me. "That's what I'm worried about." She shifted in her fur-lined boots. "Maybe," she hedged, "I could bring him into the hospital, and you could give me a few pointers?"

I looked at Katherine and realized that I could say something like, "I'm sorry but I'm not accepting any new patients right now," and snub her as she'd always done to me. Or I could accept her awkward attempt to finally make a friendly connection. I knew that Katherine could easily find the information she needed to care for Gilman's new hamster online, but for some reason she'd decided to ask me. I did what Peter would nudge me to do—I stepped forward. Or rather, I stepped up.

"Bring him by anytime, and bring Gilman along too. He should know how to care for his new pet." Kids often listen to and remember instructions that come from me rather than their parents, either because of my authoritative lab coat or because I speak in a language that both animals and young ones understand.

"Also, Brett could show Gilman a thing or two about how to care for his new pet. He had a hamster too. Now both of my boys have birds. Brett has Quinn, a cockatoo, and Luke has Lennon and Ringo."

"Lennon and Ringo, as in the Beatles?" She raised an eyebrow. "That's a throwback."

"Yeah," I said, now rolling my eyes. "Long story."

"Gilman insisted on naming his hamster 'Lil Ham,'" she grinned. We stood facing each other, and for the first time, I felt Katherine was regarding me as her equal—just two moms trying to do the best we can for our kids.

"I'll bring him in next week," she said with new familiarity. As she turned back toward her house, she stopped herself. "You know, I envy you. I used to have a career. I had my own real estate business. I was the number one realtor in lower Westchester County." I pictured Katherine in pumps, pearls, and lipstick, smiling widely on real estate signs up and down the neighborhood.

"I never intended to give it up, but after I had Gilman I got comfortable staying home. I kept saying I'd go back to work someday. Well, obviously that never happened. I just had another baby . . . "

"Taking care of kids is a full-time job," I said, feeling obliged to say something. And it was true.

"Oh, sure they keep me busy, but sometimes"—she looked over her shoulder as if someone else in the neighborhood might be listening in—"I get really bored."

I was surprised by her sudden candor but also delighted.

"Seriously, girl," she said, lowering her voice again, "my idea of excitement is the Home Shopping Network and a bottle of wine. You should join me sometime."

11:30 A.M., ANIMAL HOSPITAL

THE WAITING ROOM was peaceful and calm. Colette was sitting at the front desk writing up records while a handful of clients thumbed through glossy-covered magazines. Even Target and Stop were unusually low key. Stop quietly followed me with her big eyes as I approached the reception desk, and

Target let out the equivalent of a sigh. Were they, too, feeling a break from the intensity of the past week, or were they sensing a shift in the weather? I've always said that animals would make the best meteorologists; they instinctively know when a change is coming, often long before we do.

"Good morning," I said as I approached Colette. "Any new calls to return?"

"Here's one," she said and handed me a Post-it with a local number on it. "She wants a quote for how much it would cost to correct her rabbit's overbite with braces." She winked and added, "In hot pink, to match her teenage daughter's."

"Did you tell her to call a traditional orthodontist?"

"I'll leave that to you."

I leaned in over the front desk. "What's that you're working on?"

"Now that it's finally calmed down around here, I can focus some attention on this." She handed me a flyer. "The holidays are coming," it read in big, red block letters, "and what better time to have an adorable photo taken of you with your exotic pet for a holiday card or gift? We will be hosting a professional photo shoot at the Veterinary Center for Birds & Exotics. If you're interested, make a reservation with us in advance."

"I learned my lesson last year," she bristled. "Do you remember? No reservation, no photo."

Last December, when Colette had suggested that the hospital host a pet photo day, I'd actually laughed. "You mean, like those glossy photos we all have of our kids sitting on Santa's lap in the mall? I'm not sure our clientele will go for it."

"Are you kidding me?" she'd insisted. "Our clients will absolutely love it."

I'd all but forgotten about the event until the day I walked into a crowded waiting room full of exotic animals in detailed holiday costumes with ornamental props: twinkling lights, pet-sized stockings, teeny-tiny fir trees, and even a miniature manger scene. I was especially impressed by the chinchilla wearing angel wings, a ferret flocked with snow, and a family of eight geckos posing on the family menorah.

"I expect over one hundred animals this year," Colette nodded with certainty.

"I can't wait to see who shows up," I returned her enthusiasm. "We can start prepping for our holiday boarders too."

"The calendar's already nearly full. Only three spaces left. Maggie dropped off Sadie and Lou this morning."

Maggie was a corporate event planner who divided her time between Westchester and Manhattan, with a home in the suburbs and an apartment on the Upper East Side. In December, when holiday events are at their peak, Maggie stays in the city and boards her two Major Mitchell's cockatoos, Sadie and Lou, with us.

"I'm afraid to ask," I said to Colette. "Any special instructions this time?"

While I was accustomed to receiving a variety of special instructions for our boarders, Maggie's requests went far beyond what we routinely accommodated. I flashed back to the first time she left Sadie and Lou at the hospital.

"When they become restless and bored, I dance for them," she said.

"Dance?" Had I heard her right?

"Yes, dance! And also they go gaga for masks. Here"— she handed me a tote bursting with beads and feathers—"I brought these back from Mardi Gras. Aren't they sensational?"

I explained to Maggie as respectfully as I could that recreating a parade through the French Quarter wasn't included in our standard pet boarding service.

"You know Maggie." Colette handed me another Post-it. "She always has the most entertaining requests."

I braced for the unknown and looked down at the scribbled handwriting in Colette's hand.

"Classic holiday music dot com?" I read out loud.

"She wants you to stream it in the boarding room. Says it'll create a festive mood."

I raised an eyebrow.

"No dancing required." Colette smiled.

12:15 P.M., EXAMINATION ROOM NUMBER THREE

MY FIRST AFTERNOON appointment was Susan and Rosie, in for a check up.

Susan and her elderly guinea pig were nose to nose, affectionately nuzzling each other like old sweethearts. Susan's eyes brightened as soon as I entered the room.

"Look, Rosie," she said. "It's Dr. Hess."

"It's a pleasure to see you too." I smiled at them both. It was a relief to see Rosie looking so well and recovered from her surgery. I picked up the small brown-and-white guinea pig and ran my hand through the peach fuzz starting to grow back on the areas of skin previously covered with ulcers and dry, crusty scabs. Rosie was no longer scratching furiously at her sides with her back legs, as she had been when her skin was so inflamed by the staph infection. Instead, she lay relaxed in the towel I was cradling her in.

"Quite a change from the last time I saw you," I said to Rosie as she nuzzled me with her brunette nose.

"I wanted to bring her in for a quick checkup before we go on vacation. Keith's taking us to Hawaii for the holiday," she said. "To get away from the cold."

"Us?" I raised an eyebrow.

Susan beamed. "Rosie too."

Every once in a while the happy ending you thought impossible happens, and if anyone deserved one, it was Susan. I thought back to that fateful day when I had delivered the news that Rosie would need major surgery to treat her necrotic intestine. When Susan called her husband, Keith, to plead for the money to pay for her pet's extensive care, she'd wept at his answer. Marnie and I feared he'd said no.

"If you say 'no' to the surgery," we overheard Susan say as she choked on the words, "I'll find a way to pay for it—without you."

Marnie and I exchanged a surprised look. We hadn't anticipated Susan's burst of bravado. But then when Susan burst back into tears, we knew he'd called her bluff. She quietly hung up the phone and sank to the floor.

"I'm sorry, Susan," I said as I went to put a hand on her arm to comfort her and offer her a tissue.

She lifted her gaze and peered at Marnie and me through soaked eyes. "He said yes."

Susan never elaborated on what else Keith had said on the other end of the line, but I guessed that he had finally acknowledged that Rosie was much more to his wife than an old guinea pig and in many ways more significant in her life than he was. If he didn't start to appreciate or in some way honor their bond, he was at risk of upsetting his marriage or even losing Susan altogether. Their heated exchange reminded me of a story I'd read online about an Australian woman who had a pet crocodile that she liked to walk on a leash. When her husband gave her an ultimatum—the croc or me—she chose the animal and reportedly said, "Husbands can look after themselves."

I returned my attention to Susan. "You need a health certificate to travel with any pet on a plane, so I'm glad you brought Rosie in. I'll run a couple of general blood tests, and if everything comes back normal, then I'll issue one. Rosie looks to be in good health, so I should be able to get you what you need before your travel day. Other than the certificate, be sure also to pack food, water, and treats in her cage and cover it with a blanket to keep her warm. Guinea pigs generally travel well on planes. Although how well they do on beaches"—I winked—"I can't say."

Susan smiled. "Rosie will be happy enough if I put her cage in a sunny spot where she can take afternoon siestas."

"Sounds superb." An afternoon siesta, I thought. I did long for a few long days to relax and do nothing. Maybe I'd surprise Peter and plan a weekend getaway to one of our favorite spots—the historic town of Rhinebeck, New York, with its stunning views of the Catskill Mountains.

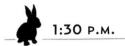 1:30 P.M.

I WANDERED BACK to the boarding room, thinking I might find Elliot in his favorite hideout, eating his lunch. There was no sign of him, but I hung around anyway, taking the opportunity to check in with our growing population of holiday boarders. I opened Flopsy's cage. As big as a dog but with huge ears and long, muscular back legs, Flopsy was a Flemish giant rabbit with reddish-brown, velvety fur and big, black, doe-like eyes. At first glance, you might mistake her for a fawn. She stretched out comfortably and yawned as I ran my hands down her back. I scratched her behind her ears, and she snuggled up further into the little nest of towels she'd made for herself. Chloe, Mr. Lombardi's mini lop-eared bunny, was in the cage next to her, also tucked into a ball of fur with her eyes closed. Chloe looked so petite compared to Flopsy. It was hard to believe that those two breeds were of the same species. Maggie's Major Mitchell's cockatoos were perched quietly in their cages, Sadie asleep and Lou watching the TV on mute. Sadie's head was tucked up under her wing, and she appeared to be leaning on Lou, who was deeply engrossed in an episode of *Clifford the Big Red Dog*. I looked at my watch. *Is it possible that I'll actually get to eat lunch before three o'clock today?* I headed out to the reception area to see who wanted to join me. I suddenly craved a savory vegetable soup. After the trauma of the past two weeks, my body could use a healthy dose of warm comfort food.

Colette looked up from the phone and raised a finger, the universal sign for "hold that thought." She returned to her conversation. "I can fit you in Monday morning at 10:30. You'll have to bring a specimen. Yes, I know, but it's not really an unusual request . . . No, we don't send someone out to do that. You'll have to do it yourself. Gloves and a ziplock bag, yes . . . That should take care of it." Colette hung up the phone and gently rubbed her temples.

She turned to me. "You were saying?"

"How does veggie soup from The Soup Stop in Mount Kisco sound?" I said cheerily. "I'll send Elliot out to pick it up. That is, if I can find him. Where is he? And for that matter," I said, looking around, "where's Marnie?"

"Said they needed to run an errand."

I looked at her suspiciously.

She shrugged and said, "I'll text Elliot and ask him to pick up lunch on the way back. You can't eat now anyway. Your next patient is waiting." She nodded toward Mrs. Irvine and her young daughter, who were watching us from their seats. I waved them back.

"Is it okay if Zadie comes with us while you examine Herman? She's fascinated by medicine."

"Absolutely," I said. I enjoyed having children come in with their pets. I held the door for mother, daughter, and Herman. Zadie proudly carried Herman, an adorable, long-haired teddy bear hamster with brown fur and a white tail, in his cage.

I closed the examination door and said, "Go ahead and take Herman out of his cage." Herman scuttled to elude Zadie's tiny hands. He hid under the paper shavings lining the bottom of his cage and then playfully poked his nose back out at her. Clearly, they played this game of chase and capture often. Zadie reached into the cage far enough to scoop him up and held Herman closely against the front of her T-shirt. I extended my hands to receive him.

"He's a wriggling one, isn't he?" I said, smiling at Zadie while securing my hold on Herman's twisting body. I flipped him over and had begun to examine his belly when Zadie whispered, "Doctor, what's that round thing?" She was pointing between Herman's tiny legs.

I looked at Mrs. Irvine for a prompt, but she was on her cell phone. "Well"—I hesitated for a moment—"those are his testicles."

She tilted her head to the side as if she were considering that. "Why are there two of them?"

Again I waited for Mrs. Irvine to answer her daughter's question, but her attention was elsewhere. I thought it was more appropriately a parent's job to explain the intricacies of the male and female anatomy, but when Zadie didn't get a response from her mother, I said, "Well, honey, they come as a pair."

"Weird," Zadie said, making a face. "I hope I don't get testicles."

I smiled. "You don't need to worry about that. Only boys have them." I remember having the testicle discussion with Brett when he was younger. He'd similarly asked me one night during bath time, "Mom, what are these?" When I'd hesitated and said, "Why don't you ask Dad about that," he'd replied, "Because you're the doctor."

"Not even one?" asked Zadie.

"Not even one." I chuckled and placed Herman back into his travel carrier. "Any more questions?" Zadie stood up and bent down close to the carrier. She leaned in and scrutinized her hamster like an expert detective.

"What's that other thing?" she said, pointing in front of Herman's testicles.

"Ahhh, well . . . "

"Oh, for goodness sake, honey." Mrs. Irvine had finally broken her attention to the phone call. "Stop asking Dr. Hess so many questions. That's his penis. He only has one of those, which is a good thing. Just one can cause a lot of problems. Ask your father."

I left Zadie and her mother to have a frank discussion about the differences between boys and girls and stepped out into the hall just as Marnie and Elliot were returning.

"There you both are. I was starting to wonder. Where were you?"

"Picking up a special guest for lunch." Marnie smiled know-ingly at Elliot. "Join us?"

I followed them back to the break room where the lunch table was set up to look like a summer picnic, a welcome jux-taposition to the gray skies outside. The table was decorated with a yellow tablecloth, and a birdcage covered in a match-ing yellow cloth sat in the middle like a centerpiece.

"What's all this?" I asked.

"Lemon's homecoming." Marnie gleamed.

I looked at Elliot for clarification. "Let me introduce you," he said, walking over to the cage, "to my new friend, Lemon." He lifted the cloth on the birdcage like a master magician. Perched in the middle was a tiny baby cockatiel covered in albino white feathers with a furry yellow crown. She let out a nearly inaudible peep.

"Oh, she's sweet," I chirped myself. "And she matches the tablecloth." I looked from Elliot to Marnie. "Very sneaky. When did this all happen?"

"Elliot told me he was hoping to adopt another cockatiel for his parents before he returned to Rhode Island," Marnie explained, "so I started looking around and found little Lemon on Petfinder."

I felt a twinge of regret. *I should have helped Elliot; instead I just worked him like a dog.* But then I quickly snapped out of my self-critical moment when little Lemon cocked her head to the side and chirped. What did it matter who helped him? The baby bird perched in front of us was adorable.

"When I saw that the breeder of this baby lived just up the road in Bedford Hills, I called on Elliot's behalf. I told her that I worked here at the hospital, and I shared some of Elliot's history with birds, about Trixie in particular, and also about his internship program. She was very impressed with his credentials and invited him up right away. She waived the requirement for personal and vet references, so long as I came along."

Elliot lured Lemon out of her cage with a pine nut. She wobbled onto his outstretched finger and happily snatched the nut from his fingers.

"She had a new flock of birds that she'd raised from birth and also hand-fed. They all looked extremely healthy," Marnie continued. "But Elliot was smitten with this one right away."

"And who wouldn't fall in love with this fuzzy little feather ball?" I said.

Lemon cocked her head and looked up at Elliot with wide eyes.

"Aren't you a pretty one?" he said and made a kissing sound.

"There he goes again," I teased, "flirting with the girls."

4:30 P.M.

I WALKED UP to Marnie as she was doing her final check on our hospitalized patients in the treatment room. "It's after four and it's Saturday. Most people aren't working at all. I think we've had a long enough week. What do you say we get out of here?"

She smiled wearily. "I was thinking the same thing. Want to walk out together?"

As soon as we stepped outside, we noticed the snow.

"Will you look at that?" Marnie said. "Fresh snow before Christmas."

"Target and Stop must have known it was coming. They were as silent as snowflakes this morning."

"It's beautiful," said Marnie.

"You know what it reminds me of?"

"Yes," she looked at me affectionately. "I do."

In a few days, it would be the anniversary of the opening of the animal hospital. What had started as a dream and a drawing I'd sketched out with my son's crayons and construction paper had become our day-to-day reality.

"It really does seem like it was just yesterday that we cut that red ribbon," Marnie said, taking the words out of my mouth.

"But then when you think of all the changes we've seen in the equipment and medicine since then, it feels like so long ago. Remember that first year it was just you and me in a sterile examination room with one pack of surgical instruments?" I said with a laugh.

"And then tiny instrument by tiny instrument we built something out of nothing," added Marnie.

"While raising our kids at the same time too. I'm not sure how we pulled that off."

"My oldest is taller than me now," Marnie tittered. She reached out and took my hand.

We walked to our cars in the dimly lit parking lot, quiet for a moment except for the accumulating snow crunching underneath our boots.

"Oh, Marnie," I sighed and gave in to sentiment. "How am I going to run this place without you? You're my second set of hands, my animal wrangler. Who's going to help me run this zoo?"

Marnie squeezed my hand.

I continued. "What am I going to do the next time Jim brings in his feisty Nile monitor? Or when Gerry brings

Harlow the hedgehog in with another 'life-threatening' condition? Who will help me then?"

"Someone with larger hands?" Marnie said, teasing.

Of course I knew I would find another technician, but no one could take Marnie's place. We knew each other so thoroughly and profoundly that we often spoke without words. The knowing glance, the affirmative nod. The unspoken bond that exists only between the closest companions.

"Marnie," I turned toward her, "I'm really going to miss you, but—I do think you're doing the right thing for your sister and for your career." I meant it. "A hospital manager position at the Los Angeles Exotics Veterinary Specialists is a very big deal. I'm really proud of you."

"That means a lot," she turned toward me. "I'm proud of you too. You've taught me so much about animal medicine and about how to be a good friend and a working mom."

I rolled my eyes. "You may be the only person in town who thinks that."

"Don't you ever doubt it." Marnie's expression turned serious. "When that nasty neighbor of yours makes you feel like you're anything less, I want you to shake it off, okay?" She said this with the same quick-fire intensity that Brett's soccer coach used on the field.

"About that," I said somewhat reluctantly. "I think Katherine and I might finally be becoming . . . friendly?"

"Are you kidding?" Marnie laughed out loud.

I looked down at the ground and nodded almost ashamedly.

"Well, there goes the neighborhood," she said and threw up her hands. "I better get out of town before things start to get really weird."

We laughed and hugged and cried until we were covered in snow from head to toe. As we drove off in different directions, I felt grateful for what many of the pet owners I'd met over the years had taught me: that the eventual loss of someone you love is worth all that you gain along the way. Marnie loved me in that rare way that our most cherished pets do—without reservation, and no matter what. I'd carry her love with me wherever our lives took us.

 **5:00 P.M., VIA VINO**

I MIRACULOUSLY ARRIVED at Via Vino on time, and I also remembered to take off my lab coat before entering the restaurant. I was feeling pretty good about myself until I saw that Peter and the boys were already there. "Over here, Mom," Brett called out and waved me to a booth in the back. Via Vino used to be a train station, and Brett and Luke have loved the spot since they were toddlers. They especially liked that they could hear the whistle outside the window as the trains pulled out of the station and that, as the cars departed, the dishes vibrated on the tables draped in red-and-white-checkered tablecloths. I slid into the booth next to Peter and squeezed his hand. "I'm so happy to be finally having a date night with *all* of my boys."

Brett was already elbow deep in the cheese plate. For his tenth birthday, we'd gone to Artisanal Fromagerie Bistro in New York City, where we had been served a complimentary starter cheese plate. Brett had been spellbound as our waiter explained the name, origin, and flavor of each wedge of cheese. To our surprise, Brett had devoured nearly the entire plate of selections. Since then, the cheese plate has been his favorite item on any menu, and after ordering dozens of them, he knows enough about cheese to impress most connoisseurs. Really, how many thirteen-year-olds actually know the origin of Mimolette Edam or Boerenkaas Gouda? Luke doesn't have the same appreciation for a cheesy starter course; he holds out for dessert. But tonight Luke was giving each cheese an honest taste before he tried to convince his older brother that a dribble of hot sauce—his condiment of choice for everything— would improve its "complexity."

Snuggled into our cozy booth in the back, we had an unobstructed view out the picture-frame front window of bedraggled commuters coming home on the Metro-North train. I relaxed into Peter's side with my glass of sauvignon blanc and felt time slow down. I released my responsibility to the pregnant pigs, geriatric ferrets, and eighty-six-pound boa constrictors and appreciated that in this moment, I was just Laurie—wife, friend, and mother. I looked into the familiar faces of Peter, Brett, and Luke and felt my heart swell with appreciation for them, and I recognized their unconditional love for me. I've learned to accept that I'll probably always relate better to animals than people; however, around this cozy family table, I'll always fit in. I closed my eyes and counted my many blessings. And maybe, if I was exceptionally blessed, tomorrow I might enjoy a day of peace and quiet before the rat race began again.

EXOTIC PET RESOURCES

Birds: Association of Avian Veterinarians (http://www.aav.org)

Reptiles: Association of Reptile and Amphibian Veterinarians (http://www.arav.org)

Reptiles and amphibians: Melissa Kaplan's Herp Care Collection (http://www.anapsid.org)

Small mammals (e.g., rabbits, ferrets, guinea pigs, chinchillas, hamsters, rats, mice, gerbils, and so forth): Association of Exotic Mammal Veterinarians (http://www.aemv.org)

Rabbits: House Rabbit Society (http://www.rabbit.org)

Ferrets: American Ferret Association (http://www.ferret.org)

Sugar gliders: Association of Sugar Glider Veterinarians (http://www.asgv.org)

Potbellied pigs: North American Potbellied Pig Association (http://www.pigs.com)

Hedgehogs: International Hedgehog Association (http://www.hedgehogclub.com)

Guinea pigs: Guinea Lynx (http://www.guinealynx.info)

Rats and mice: Rat & Mouse Club of America (http://www.rmca.org)

ABOUT THE AUTHORS

PHOTO: JAMIE KILGORE

DR. LAURIE HESS, one of only approximately 125 bird specialists in the world, founded the Veterinary Center for Birds & Exotics in 2010 because she wanted to offer exotic pets and their owners a truly unique medical facility that caters only to the specialized needs of exotic species. The center provides comprehensive, cutting-edge care for birds and exotic pets, utilizing state-of-the-art technology—including digital X-rays, ultrasonography, endoscopy, laser, and electrosurgery—and offers the comprehensive care of a large hospital within the personalized setting of a small one. It is the only American Animal Hospital Association–accredited bird and exotic specialty referral hospital in New York (treating patients from New York, New Jersey, Connecticut, and

Pennsylvania) and only one of seven such hospitals in the United States and Canada. It is also the only hospital in Westchester County, New York, and surrounding areas that offers emergency phone consultations 24/7/365 for birds and exotic pets.

Laurie graduated summa cum laude, Phi Beta Kappa, from Yale University and received her doctorate in veterinary medicine from Tufts University. She completed a one-year internship and two-year residency at the prestigious Animal Medical Center in New York City, where she stayed on to head the Avian & Exotic Pet Service for more than a decade, before opening her own specialized practice. When Laurie isn't at her animal hospital, she's at home in Mount Kisco, New York, with her husband and two sons and the rest of their family: Ringo and Lennon, Gloster canaries; Quinn, a Goffin's cockatoo; Dale, a blue-headed pionus parrot; and Bingo, Gizmo, Bean, and Tilly, a menagerie of cats.

SAMANTHA ROSE is an Emmy Award–winning television producer, author, and a multi-best-selling coauthor of nearly a dozen nonfiction projects in the areas of health and wellness, diet, lifestyle, how-to, parenting, and memoir.

ACKNOWLEDGMENTS

YEARS AGO, WHEN a client off-handedly commented to me that I had so many fascinating stories of animal owners and their pets that I should write a memoir, I never imagined that I would actually do it. Many drafts later, I could not be prouder of the memoir that *Unlikely Companions* has become, and I could not be more grateful to the many people who have supported and encouraged me along the way.

First of all, to my cowriter, Samantha Rose, I am tremendously thankful. Without her patience, persistence, and belief in our project, we would not have the final version of this narrative, as we dreamed it would be several years ago. Her masterful writing and professionalism are unrivaled and made working with her more fun than work. Samantha truly captured my voice in this book and told my story in my own words.

Next, I want to thank my literary agent, Yfat Reiss Gendell, for her undying support and encouragement through this labor of love. At every step on the path to publication,

Yfat's reassurance that we would, in fact, reach the end, was truly a comfort. Special thanks, too, to Yfat's Editorial Associate Jessica Felleman for answering all of my communications throughout the publishing process. I am honored that such an esteemed group as Foundry Literary & Media was willing to take on my project, and I attribute so much of the success of *Unlikely Companions* to Yfat and her team.

In addition, I want to recognize our incredibly talented editor, Renée Sedliar, and her group at Da Capo Press, for making our book even better. Samantha Rose and I commented repeatedly, after receiving Renée's edits, how she truly understood what we were trying to convey in the book and simply helped us say it best. I knew from the first conversation I had with Renée and her group that they were animal lovers and really "got it." Special thanks to Editorial Assistant Miriam Riad for helping Renée shepherd this project along so smoothly, to Production Editor Cisca Schreefel for keeping the trains running on time in production, and to Director of Publicity Lissa Warren for falling in love with a veterinarian's story, supporting Renée in bringing me to Da Capo, and of course, for being such an animal lover herself. In addition, thanks to Publisher John Radziewicz and his team member Justin Lovell for supporting this project from the start, to Director of the Art Department Alex Camlin for connecting us with Cover Designer Kerry Rubenstein, who created the most beautiful book cover I have ever seen, and to copy editor Jennifer Kelland Fagan for making us all look better than we could hope to in print. I also want to acknowledge Kevin Hanover and his marketing team at Da Capo for his invaluable advice and guidance in helping me connect this book with the people who love the animals that exotic vets like me care for every day. The enthusiasm and collective efforts of the Da Capo team have been overwhelming.

Of course, I want to thank my wonderful family for their never-ending patience with me through both the development of my veterinary career and the writing of this book. To my parents, I thank you for enabling me to accomplish my dream of becoming a veterinarian by putting me through veterinary school. To my husband, Peter, and to my kids, Brett and Luke, I thank you for putting up with my long nights at the animal hospital, missed family events, and dinners interrupted by emergency calls to treat critically ill pets. Without all of your support, I would not have been able to open the Veterinary Center for Birds & Exotics and would not have this marvelous memoir.

In addition, I want to acknowledge my terrific staff—doctors, veterinary technicians and assistants, receptionists, and managers—at the Veterinary Center for Birds & Exotics, without whom I could not run the animal hospital. I spend more time with all of you than I do anyone else, and I am in awe of your talents. Thank you for helping me build our unique veterinary hospital upon which this memoir is based.

Finally, I want to thank all of the pet owners and their animals whom I have treated over the past two decades. To the literally thousands of clients whose lives I have been fortunate to touch during my career so far as a veterinarian, I thank you for entrusting me with the care of your precious pets and for giving me the stories that make up the memoir of *Unlikely Companions*. Just as I hope I have impacted all of you in some little way, you, too have impacted me and have made me the veterinarian I am today. Thank you for letting me into your lives and for sharing all of your friends feathered, furred, and scaled.